LATE NIGHT EXTRA

ALISTAIR BROWN

CHRISTIAN FOCUS PUBLICATIONS

©1991 ALISTAIR BROWN
Published by
Christian Focus Publications Ltd
Geanies House, Fearn, Ross-shire,
IV20 1TW, Scotland, Great Britain.

Printed and bound in Great Britain
by Cox & Wyman Ltd, Reading

All Scripture quotations are from
the New International Version,
published by Hodder and Stoughton.

Cover picture courtesy of
Highland and Islands Enterprise.

Cover design by Seoris N. Mcgillivray.

CONTENTS

SUBJECTS
(in alphabetical order)

ASSURANCE	11;18;23;29;60
CHRISTMAS	25
THE CHURCH	21;26;45
EASTER	30
ENDURANCE	10;45;54
FAITH	15;20;32;50
FAITHFULNESS	3;6;19;37
FORGIVENESS	5;7;13;46
GOD	1;15;23;42;43;44;56
GODLINESS	35;53
THE GOSPEL	4;6;9;14;17;30;36;58;59
GUIDANCE	23;33;40;58
HOPE	5;33
HUMILITY	5;8
JOY	2
JUDGMENT	28;47;53;57
LEADERSHIP	41;52
LOVE	43;46;60
MARRIAGE/FAMILY	24;51
PRAISE/WORSHIP	27;38;55
PRAYER	22;34;49
SERVICE	12;16;29;36
SPIRITUAL GROWTH	31;34;35;52;54;55
STEWARDSHIP	16;39
WITNESSING	12;20;29;32;48

INTRODUCTION

This collection of epilogues can be used for entirely private purposes, perhaps as a short devotional study at the beginning or end of the day. Or it can be an aid for leading a group. For either purpose I have tried to set down relevant topics taken from a wide range of scripture passages. Certain main themes recur, but they do that in the Bible as well and it is right to give them extra emphasis.

Those who read these epilogues for their own private study will find the extra Bible readings (noted at the end of each epilogue) particularly worth pursuing. These 'secondary' passages are always related to the main theme, but they may look at the topic from a different angle, offering a richer understanding of the subject.

If you regularly have to speak to others, perhaps you will find some fresh resources in these pages. For simplicity the biblical text is included (New International Version), although you may find it more helpful to ask someone else to read the relevant passage from his own Bible. Thereafter I would hope that you would take what is written here only as a tool. While it may offer a framework for what you say, your talk will be richer if you also bring in your own insights and illustrations.

Whatever your reason for using this book, I trust it is enjoyable to read and gives you some greater knowledge of our God.

Alistair Brown

1
SNAPSHOT OF GOD
(Deuteronomy 32:4)

He is the Rock, his works are perfect, and all his ways are just.
A faithful God who does no wrong, upright and just is he.

A few people in biblical times had very direct encounters with God (e.g., Abraham, Genesis 18:1; Moses, Exodus 33:11,18-23; Isaiah, Isaiah 6:1). If only these people had had cameras with which to photograph what they saw of God. They didn't, and in any case it would have done them little good: a) because his majesty would have been too bright and glorious for even the best of today's colour films to register; b) because God is spirit (without physical form in the sense in which we know it), so no picture would have been possible.

Nevertheless, these people did have a picture of God, and this verse gives it to us in words rather than on film. With photographs, no one snapshot fully captures a person's likeness. Neither does any one verse of the Bible, but through key words here we 'see' a very great deal of what God is like.

Rock. Children at the seaside enjoy leaping from rock to rock embedded in the sand, confident of a sure foothold with stones which may weigh tons. And a rock-like God conveys the image of stability. In a world where one century has seen more innovation and inventions than all other centuries put together, God doesn't change. Therefore, those who know him and have their lives entrusted to his care have a security unknown to others.

Perfect. Not only is this word used, but later in the verse it's said that God does no wrong, and that he is upright. These terms combine to picture God as morally without fault. We're not used to perfection, either in people or things. For example, we might long for a perfectly made car engine. If it were flawless we could be assured of thousands of miles of trouble free motoring. But because the engine is not perfect, inevitably the faults will show up some day, leaving us stranded in pouring rain miles from anywhere. God is perfect, however, and his actions are always consistent with that nature. A tree with no blemish will produce fruit with no blemish. And there is nothing in God which could lead to him acting wrongly. Our faith and confidence in him must grow when we realise that our God never makes mistakes.

Just. One example of a perfect God at work is that every judgment he makes will be just. The writer is so sure of this he repeats the point later in the verse for emphasis. A just God will never overlook essential facts. Nor need anyone fear bias, as if God had any special favourites from one race, social class, or educational background. All his creation are equal before him: equally loved, and equally judged. Should the outcome of that judgment be unpleasant, then that reflects only on our sinful living against God and his laws. He cannot be accused of treating us unfairly. What God does will always be just.

Faithful. One of the obscure words theologians apply to God is 'immutable'. All it means is that he never changes. He never grows old; he never takes moods; he never thinks one thing one day and another the next. God is always the same. Therefore, for example, no-one should worry that God will suddenly stop loving him. People are fickle, and may 'go off' someone. But God is utterly consistent. Day after day, year after year, whether we're good or bad, God's love stays the same. That isn't a licence to sin, as if it didn't matter, because no-one concerned to please God will ever want to disobey and sadden him. But it is a reassurance that his love is not dependent on our goodness. Even though we fail, even though we fall short of our own standards never mind God's, yet he is true toward us. Because he is faithful his love and kindness will never alter nor run out.

So here is a picture of God. Many a man carries a photograph around constantly to remind him of the one he loves. Perhaps he keeps it in an inside pocket to be near his heart. Here is a snapshot worth carrying so we never forget what God is like, this one worth carrying in our hearts.

Read also: Psalm 18:1-3

2
REASONS TO REJOICE
(Luke 24:44-53)

⁴⁴He said to them, "This is what I told you while I was still with you: Everything must be fulfilled that is written about me in the Law of Moses, the Prophets and the Psalms."

⁴⁵Then he opened their minds so they could understand the Scriptures. ⁴⁶He told them, "This is what is written: The Christ will suffer and rise from the dead on the third day, ⁴⁷and repentance and forgiveness of sins will be preached in his name to all nations, beginning at Jerusalem. ⁴⁸You are witnesses of these things. ⁴⁹I am going to send you what my Father has promised; but stay in the city until you have been clothed with power from on high."

⁵⁰When he had led them out to the vicinity of Bethany, he lifted up his hands and blessed them. ⁵¹While he was blessing them, he left them and was taken up into heaven. ⁵²Then they worshipped him and returned to Jerusalem with great joy. ⁵³And they stayed continually at the temple, praising God.

A stranger arrives in town. He wants a great time. He jumps into a taxi and tells the driver, "Take me somewhere I'll really enjoy myself. I want to be among happy people who'll make me feel good." What are the odds that he'll be driven to a church? Not high. Christians don't have a reputation for being people of infectious joy.

Yet the second last verse of Luke's gospel (verse 52) says that these apostles were filled with great joy as they returned to Jerusalem. They'd probably never been happier. What makes that even more remarkable is the timing

- Jesus had only just been taken from them. If a soldier found himself left alone in the trenches to face the enemy, all his comrades gone, he wouldn't be rejoicing overmuch. But these disciples were joyful, even though their greatest and most powerful ally had disappeared.

Why, at this of all times, did these Christians feel so good?

1) Because now they understood the gospel message. These men had been with Jesus for some three years, yet during that time they had had great difficulty grasping what his ministry was really about. At first they may have regarded him as only a remarkable teacher, a courageous reformer, a miraculous prophet, or a charismatic leader. In time they realised he was much more. But even when Peter had the insight that Jesus was the Messiah (Matthew 16:16), he was probably expecting Jesus to become a warrior Saviour who would sweep the Roman oppressors from the land. When Jesus spoke instead of being put to death Peter rebuked him. In turn that brought from Jesus the sharpest reply he ever gave any man: "Get behind me, Satan! You are a stumbling-block to me; you do not have in mind the things of God, but the things of men" (Matthew 16:23). Poor Peter didn't understand that Jesus 'wanted' to die, and his confusion was shared by them all.

But now they did know. Luke records that in these last days with the disciples "he opened their minds so they could understand" (verse 45). He talked to them about his death and resurrection, and linked that with repentance and forgiveness of sins (verses 46-47). Perhaps for the first time they realised that Jesus had chosen to die in order to free them from sin. What they had thought to be the world's greatest tragedy, they saw now as the world's greatest act of love. Therefore they had joy.

2) Because now they had the promise of the Holy Spirit. These men would have been devastated if they had thought they really were being abandoned. As well as feeling very vulnerable, they'd also have wondered how they could possibly do what Jesus was asking of them. There are few experiences more frustrating or frightening than having work to do but lacking the skill or tools to do it. Jesus' reference about preaching to all nations (verse 47) would have had those effects on them if they'd believed they were being left to get on with witnessing to the world in their own power.

But negative reactions were avoided because Jesus was guaranteeing them God's power. Speaking of the Holy Spirit, he told them, "I am going to send you what my Father has promised; but stay in the city until you have been clothed with power from on high" (verse 49). His words must have thrilled them for three reasons:

a) *God's promise had been given.* There were no "mights" or "maybes" here. God had said this gift of the Spirit would be their equipment. Because a promise is as good as the person who makes it, they knew this gift was for sure. God's word was certain.

b) *God's promise was power from on high.* That's the same power they had seen in Jesus. His miracles, life of prayer, self-discipline, and wise teaching - his whole character and ministry - came entirely from the Holy Spirit. That power would soon be on them. This made realistic everything they were being asked to do.

c) *God's promise was to be clothed with power from on high.* The imagery of being clothed carries the sense of complete covering. These disciples would not have only a temporary touch of power which might wear off. Nor would just part of their lives be affected. Rather, they were to be wrapped round with the Spirit as a huge blanket envelops a young child. Every part of their being and every part of their work would be different.

Jesus might be leaving them in respect of his physical person. But, in a more intimate way than ever, he would still be with them by the Spirit to make the new ministry possible. Therefore there was joy.

3) Because now they had Jesus' blessing. He was giving that blessing as he was taken from their eyes (verses 50-51). Luke doesn't describe the blessing. There are no details of what Jesus said. However, to have received any blessing must at least have told these men they were in the will of God.

That's what they needed to know. Perhaps they guessed that great struggles lay ahead. They could have little naivety about the opposition they would face since only weeks before they had seen Jesus himself nailed to a cross. But even in the devastation of a tornado there is one place of dead calm: right in the middle. There may be havoc on all sides, but in the centre there is peace. These apostles knew now that the only place of peace for them was in the will of God. Ahead and around them would still lie trial and trouble, but if they were right with God they would be safe in respect of the things that really mattered. Christ's blessing convinced them they were in that will, and so they had joy.

The Holy Spirit's fruit in each Christian includes joy (Galatians 5:22). Those who have missed out on joy may have done so because they never realised the grounds they had for rejoicing through the gospel, the power of the Spirit, and the blessing of Jesus.

Read also: Philippians 4:4-9

3
THE PROMISE
(Matthew 28:18-20)

18Then Jesus came to them and said, "All authority in heaven and on earth has been given to me. 19Therefore go and make disciples of all nations, baptising them in the name of the Father and of the Son and of the Holy Spirit, 20and teaching them to obey everything I have commanded you. And surely I am with you always, to the very end of the age."

When parents tell their children such-and-such will happen, the children may ask, "Do you promise?" They reckon a promise won't be broken. Jesus gave an unbreakable promise in verse 20: "I am with you always, to the very end of the age." There are three things which make it special.

1) **The one giving the promise.** Who was to be with these disciples? Was it the Roman army, the Jewish authorities, fellow Christians, legions of angels? It was none of these, but Jesus himself: "*I* am with you always." The same person they had seen heal the sick, raise the dead, drive out demons, give the blind sight and the deaf hearing, this Jesus would be with them.

That's what made all the difference when it came to accepting the command to evangelise (known as 'The Great Commission'). Little children panic if left alone. Many can't cope with being upstairs if Mum or Dad is downstairs. To feel secure they need someone strong and trustworthy with them. Alone these disciples could do nothing. But with Jesus beside them all things were possible. The difference was because of who was with them.

2) Those to whom the promise is made. Some find it hard to believe a promise applies to them. They're sure it's real for others, but it could never be true for them. But here Jesus says specifically, "I am with *you* always."

No parent would tell his children, "I'll take you all to the zoo today," and then, as they reach the gates, turn to one and say, "But I didn't mean you, only the others." If no parent would do that, how much less would Jesus miss out any of his children? The promise of his presence applies to all who are disciples. It's special because not one is missed out.

3) The extent of the promise. When we make a promise it is usually for one occasion and that occasion only. This promise of Jesus, however, is for ever and for all situations: "I am with you *always*."

Would Jesus be with his disciples one year on, twenty years on? Always. Would he be beside them if they were on trial before rulers? Always. Would he be alongside if they were suffering persecution? Always. Would he be there if they were sad, sick, or anxious? Always. Would he be close even if they let him down? Always.

There is no qualifying of this promise with regard to time or circumstance. Jesus said he'd be with them through whatever was happening, right until the very end of the age. Since that end hasn't come yet, present day disciples are as assured of the presence of their Lord as these first believers. This is a promise without limits. Its power never runs out.

Since we have such a promise of Jesus' presence, is there anything in life the Christian cannot face? Is there any challenge, difficulty, burden, or task too great? Nothing's impossible if he's there. And he is. He promised it.

Read also: Exodus 33:12-17

4
WHITE AS SNOW
(Isaiah 1:18)

"Come now, let us reason together," says the Lord. "Though your sins are like scarlet, they shall be as white as snow; though they are red as crimson, they shall be like wool."

Most men know what it's like to get a drop of blood on an immaculate white shirt. Perhaps a tiny cut from shaving that morning has opened again. Against the best white a washing powder can produce, that drop of crimson blood stands out brightly. And even a man of confidence and assurance feels self-conscious when that happens. He knows everyone he meets will notice.

That scenario highlights the fact that there are hardly any colours more garish than scarlet or crimson. None could be in greater contrast to white, especially the white of snow or wool. Therefore God uses these when he wants to illustrate the extent of his mercy to men.

Yes, their sins are terrible. Sometimes people evaluate their lives leniently, excusing much that they do. God, however, is holy and pure, and wants comparable behaviour from men (Matthew 5:48). Sadly all fall far short of that standard (Romans 3:23). Thus, in God's eyes man's sins are like scarlet or crimson.

"Yet," he says, "they won't stay like that. I'll make them white as snow or wool." The change is immense. As great as the contrast between these vivid colours and white, equally great will be the contrast between a person's old life and new. Before he was dreadfully guilty; now he's completely forgiven.

With God, then, even the worst of sinners has hope. No matter how terrible his wrongs, he is not beyond God's love or power to save. Instead of being stained by past sins, his life can become as white as snow.

Read also: 2 Corinthians 5:21

5
HOPE FOR HONEST FAILURES
(Luke 18:9-14)

⁹To some who were confident of their own righteousness and looked down on everybody else, Jesus told this parable: ¹⁰"Two men went up to the temple to pray, one a Pharisee and the other a tax collector. ¹¹The Pharisee stood up and prayed about himself: 'God, I thank you that I am not like other men - robbers, evildoers, adulterers - or even like this tax collector. ¹²I fast twice a week and give a tenth of all I get.'

¹³"But the tax collector stood at a distance. He would not even look up to heaven, but beat his breast and said, 'God, have mercy on me, a sinner.'

¹⁴"I tell you that this man, rather than the other, went home justified before God. For everyone who exalts himself will be humbled, and he who humbles himself will be exalted."

No-one can know today whether Jesus used drama when telling his parables. It isn't hard, though, to imagine him putting on the airs and graces of an arrogant Pharisee and speaking that man's words in a superior voice. Perhaps Jesus' listeners were in fits of laughter at the portrayal, the laughter also of recognition that here was a very possible scenario.

Of course Jesus wasn't out to amuse but to teach. What he had to say here was that God was ready to accept honest confessions of failure but could never receive those who came proclaiming themselves to be good. Two things stand out.

1) The Pharisee's mistake. His problem began with his point of comparison. In his prayer he mentioned robbers, evildoers, adulterers and the tax collector cowering in the corner. Since they were all known deceivers, it wasn't hard for the Pharisee to come to the conclusion that he was better than any of them.

But what did that really prove? Any woman who despairs of her ability to run her home can cheer herself up by choosing to visit a neighbour notorious for her disorganisation and untidiness. Yet does that make her own homemaking all right? Is someone with a broken leg to be thought well simply because the man next door is in a worse condition with a broken neck? These 'horizontal' comparisons with people worse than us don't make us good.

The Pharisee's mistake was to evaluate his life that way, combined with the assumption that he'd pleased God by carrying out religious observances such as fasting and tithing. He didn't realise that God was looking at his heart, looking for humility and love rather than pride and ritual service. He failed to see he didn't match God's real standards. Since he didn't see his sin, he neither acknowledged nor confessed it, and so he was not forgiven.

2) The tax-collector's success. His success in finding forgiveness had nothing to do with a good life. It was wrong before God and man. Tax-collectors usually made their living by what they could extract from people over and above what they passed on to the authorities. People knew they were being over-charged but were powerless to stop it. Add to that the fact that these men were in the service of the hated Roman occupying army, and it's easy to see why they were despised. Jesus had picked a tough category to illustrate how someone could be justified before God.

But Jesus' point was that forgiveness has nothing to do

with merit in the life of an individual. This tax-collector had none. His life was sinful. The man's success in finding justification was that he knew how bad he was, confessed it, and called out for mercy. He didn't pretend he was anything other than what he was, a miserable sinner. He could only acknowledge that and plead for forgiveness.

And, Jesus said, he got it. The tax-collector had humbled himself before God, and would therefore be exalted. The Pharisee had tried to exalt himself and so would be humbled.

Therefore there is hope with God for all except the proud. Those who are honest failures will find forgiveness if they confess and turn from their sin. God is a God of mercy to those who come seeking.

Read also: Ephesians 2:8-9

6
CONSEQUENCES
(2 Timothy 2:11-13)

¹¹Here is a trustworthy saying:
  If we died with him,
  we will also live with him;
¹²if we endure,
  we will also reign with him.
If we disown him,
  he will also disown us;
¹³if we are faithless,
  he will remain faithful,
  for he cannot disown himself.

One of the earliest truths any child learns is that actions have consequences. If Jenny won't eat her tea, then her mother gets angry. If Johnny won't go to bed when told, then his father may warm his rear quarters. Despite these examples, consequences of actions are not always unpleasant. Good things flow from obedience, tidiness, effort, and so on.

Here is one place where Paul (probably borrowing the words of an early hymn) uses this principle of "if...then" in order to teach Timothy some fundamental truths about the Christian faith.

1) If we died with him, we will also live with him. These words could originate from Jesus' strict terms of discipleship: "For whoever wants to save his life will lose it, but whoever loses his life for me will save it" (Luke 9:24). Or Paul may be recalling his own words, "...if we died with

Christ, we believe that we will also live with him" (Romans 6:8).

Whatever thought was in the background, Paul is telling Timothy the essential truth that the new life with Jesus can only be experienced if the old life has become forgiven history. No man can enjoy marriage without firmly and finally letting go of singleness and all its trappings. Old sins must have gone with Jesus on the cross if resurrection freedom is to be a reality.

2) If we endure, we will also reign with him. What would happen to you if you tried to run a four minute mile? Off goes the starter's gun and muscles are galvanised into action. Round the track your legs pound, but those muscles aren't used to exercise greater than the short walk from office desk to cafeteria or from car park to supermarket. By lap two the pain has begun; by lap three it's excruciating; and lap four never comes because those legs have gone on strike. The spirit was willing, but the flesh was very, very weak. No medals for you!

And Paul sees a correspondence between endurance as a Christian and a share in Christ's victory. Jesus' death alone brings forgiveness, but forgiven sinners must persevere in discipleship in the face of whatever troubles, temptations, battles, and failures come along. To overcome these Paul believed he had to "Run in such a way as to get the prize", and that required discipline and training (1 Corinthians 9:24-25). Entrance into discipleship may be free, but the pace is still hard. It's only with endurance that the finishing line is reached.

3) If we disown him, he will also disown us. Taken at face value this statement offends many. They don't like the idea that Jesus would turn anyone away. They want to believe that heaven's doors are open wide to all, no matter whether the person has given devoted love to Christ or blasphemous denial of him.

But that is to believe in a plasticine god, one we have pressed and prodded, moulded and shaped into an image to suit our wishes. Rather, Paul's teaching here (and elsewhere) is that if someone has chosen to reject Jesus in this life then that is completed by Jesus granting him a reciprocal rejection in the next. Jesus' own words were clear: "Whoever acknowledges me before men, I will also acknowledge him before my Father in heaven. But whoever disowns me before men, I will disown him before my Father in heaven" (Matthew 10:32-33).

If that seems harsh, it may be because man's inner pride tells him he shouldn't need a Saviour. Imagine a man who boasted he has never needed to consult a doctor. He has always shrugged off any illness after a few days. But then he falls sick. This time he's seriously ill, and everyone can see his life is fading. Concerned friends bring a doctor to him, but the man will pay him no heed. He doesn't want treatment. Nevertheless, the physician is able to diagnose the condition and prescribes medication which will bring a cure. But, in his arrogance, the sick man continues to boast he has no need of doctors and does nothing with the prescription. Before long he is dead. He denied the physician. By his own choice, therefore, benefit from the physician's medicine was denied to him.

4) If we are faithless, he will remain faithful, for he cannot disown himself. With the previous point there was harmony between man's behaviour and God's. This time there is discord. God acts differently from man. We are faithless but he is faithful.

Yet this seems strange coming immediately after the statement that if we disown him he will also disown us.

However, the difference between the man who 'disowns' and the man who is 'faithless' is not one of degree but of type. What is spoken of here is not the faithlessness of the unbeliever, but the foolish waywardness of a disciple whose heart is fundamentally right with God. He means to please his Lord, but sometimes he fails.

Jesus used an illustration of two roads. One was of motorway proportions with many on it all heading for destruction. The other was more like a narrow country lane, full of twists and turns, but leading to eternal life. There is all the difference in the world between the people who travel these roads. The broad road has a large crowd, all cruising carelessly and comfortably to hell. The narrow road carries much less traffic, though the destination is good. Those Paul is speaking about as 'faithless' are among the smaller number on the 'B' road. They're individuals picking their way along a difficult and treacherous path, unwisely leaving that track from time to time and falling into potholes and ditches. Thankfully their stupidity and badness in going off the road does not annul God's goodness. His unchanging nature is to love, and out of that great love, he's willing to pull them back. "If we confess our sins, he is faithful and just and will forgive us our sins and purify us from all unrighteousness" (1 John 1:9).

Too often the devil convinces us we are failed Christians and there's no future for us. That's his lie. It's not God's opinion. He never loved us initially because we were good (for we weren't!); our failures now neither catch him by surprise nor put him off. We do not cease to be his sons even when we disappoint him. He is our heavenly Father and that never changes. Therefore, even when we are faithless he remains faithful.

Read also: Hebrews 12:1-3

7
SEEKING MERCY
(Psalm 51:1-4)

¹Have mercy on me, O God,
according to your unfailing love;
according to your great compassion
blot out my transgressions.
²Wash away all my iniquity
and cleanse me from my sin.

³For I know my transgressions,
and my sin is always before me.
⁴Against you, you only, have I sinned
and done what is evil in your sight,
so that you are proved right when you speak
and justified when you judge.

This Psalm is set against a background of adultery and murder. King David had made Bathsheba pregnant, and then tried to cover up his wrongdoing by deliberately having her husband, Uriah, put in the front line of battle so that he was killed. But Nathan, a prophet, exposed his sin leaving David crying out now for God's mercy. (The full story is in 2 Samuel 11 and 12.)

In these verses his appeal for forgiveness involves the recognition of three key aspects of God's mercy.

1) Recognition that he had sinned. Pride prevents some from ever admitting they are wrong. They'd argue that black was white rather than accept they have faults. Not David. Perhaps before Nathan came to him he'd tried to suppress his guilt, but not now. Verse 3 has his clear confession: "I know my transgressions, and my sin is always before me." His actions haunted him, and now he admits to God how wrong they were.

That's the essential first stage. A doctor cannot treat someone who won't accept he's ill. If the person won't believe anything is wrong he's not going to take the medication. Admission of sin is equally necessary before any cure to it can be applied.

2) Recognition that he had sinned against God. David's confession and appeal for mercy are directed to God because he realises that God is the one offended. David is so conscious of that he emphasises it specially in verse 4: "Against you, you only, have I sinned and done what is evil in your sight."

At a human level, David, as King, had no-one to fear. He was the law maker and enforcer in the land. No-one was a judge over him. If it pleased him he could put a hundred men in the front line of battle and sleep with all their wives. David was answerable to no man. But now he accepts he's answerable to God, and his actions towards Bathsheba and Uriah were shameful and wrong. No man could judge David, but his Maker and Lord could and did, and David was found guilty (verse 4).

Many today imagine that they can please themselves. The foundation of much morality is, 'It's all right as long as no-one gets hurt'. Sometimes it goes one stage further, 'It's all right as long as no-one finds out'. What David discovered was that God has standards to be met and he holds us accountable to them, whether or not our actions are known or acceptable to others. Recognising that we've hurt God, and therefore it's to him we must go for forgiveness, is the essential second stage to finding mercy.

3) Recognition that nothing could save him now except God's mercy. By the time this prayer was spoken, David had realised how wrong he'd been, and he'd no intention of repeating his actions. But that wasn't enough. That didn't remove his sin. A prisoner jailed for serious crimes isn't set free even if he knows how bad he's been, or if he's polite and kind now to his guards and fellow inmates. Likewise neither David's recognition of wronging God nor his new and better life eradicated his guilt from the past.

Since David's offence was against God, only God could release him from his guilt. And that would be an act of sheer mercy. David knew God as One with "unfailing love" and "great compassion" (verse 1). A God like that was not out to get him, not looking to send him to hell. Such a God would not despise "a broken and contrite heart" (verse 17). So he pleads for cleansing from his sin (verse 2) on the basis of the mercy of a loving God (verse 1).

And he received that mercy. Even after such a terrible episode in his life, David was forgiven. Many years later God called David one who "followed me with all his heart" (1 Kings 14:8). That description reveals the extent of his forgiveness. Nothing less than the same utter cleansing from sin is available still for anyone who will seek God's mercy.

Read also: 1 John 1:8-2:2

8
INFLATED EGOS
(Matthew 18:1-5)

[1] At that time the disciples came to Jesus and asked, "Who is the greatest in the kingdom of heaven?"

[2] He called a little child and had him stand among them. [3] And he said: "I tell you the truth, unless you change and become like little children, you will never enter the kingdom of heaven. [4] Therefore, whoever humbles himself like this child is the greatest in the kingdom of heaven.

[5] And whoever welcomes a little child like this in my name welcomes me..."

What makes someone great? We have several routes to greatness today. Power is one. A president, prime minister, or even a trade union leader is considered great because of the number of people he commands. Sometimes greatness is based on talent. Some are reckoned great footballers, great pianists, or great singers. Another way of attributing greatness is because of looks. Sport or pop music pin ups have fans swooning at their feet because they're 'gorgeous'. Intellect can be another means by which someone is thought to be great. He has great ideas, insights, philosophies.

Jesus rejects all these as a basis for greatness. When the disciples asked him who was the greatest in the kingdom of heaven, Jesus replied that even to enter that kingdom a person had to be like a little child. That doesn't mean someone should become childish, but he must be childlike.

What characteristics of children are important for the

kingdom of heaven? Three stand out.

1) Simplicity. There is no merit in being naive or simplistic, but the person fit for the kingdom of heaven will use his knowledge and experience to direct him to simple faith. He will believe what is obvious and right to believe. He will not allow selfishness or prejudice to decide what he will think.

2) Trust. A child asks his parents, "Can I have my supper now?" He isn't questioning whether or not there will be supper, only when he can have it. He knows his parents love him. They will provide. He trusts.

3) Humility. Jesus drew attention to this quality especially (verse 4). Little children are only too well aware of their weakness and vulnerability. At a swimming pool, one father teased his infant son. As he held his boy in his arms he walked steadily into deeper water. The colour drained from the lad's face, and he clung on more and more tightly to Dad. He knew he had to. If his father dropped him he had no way to survive. A child cannot afford pride. Admitting his weakness is his only way to life.

Jesus' message is that there's no room in the kingdom of heaven for inflated egos. Only those who come simply, with trust, and in humility can enter. And, he says, all who come like that are great in God's kingdom.

Read also: Romans 8:12-17

9
THE GIFT OF THE GOSPEL
(John 3:16-21)

¹⁶For God so loved the world that he gave his one and only Son that whoever believes in him shall not perish but have eternal life. ¹⁷For God did not send his Son into the world to condemn the world, but to save the world through him. ¹⁸Whoever believes in him is not condemned, but whoever does not believe stands condemned already because he has not believed in the name of God's one and only Son. ¹⁹This is the verdict: Light has come into the world, but men loved darkness instead of light because their deeds were evil. ²⁰Everyone who does evil hates the light, and will not come into the light for fear that his deeds will be exposed. ²¹But whoever lives by the truth comes into the light, so that it may be seen plainly that what has been done has been done through God.

Verse 16 is perhaps the best known in the whole Bible, and it's a verse all about God.

1) It tells of God's love. The starting point of the Christian story - of the gospel - is that God loves this world. It would be easy to understand if he didn't. Mankind has so turned his back on God, broken his law, and refused his mercy, that God would be perfectly just if he was against man. Some feel he is. They think of him as a God of vengeance, out to punish every wrong - like a sadistic school-teacher, searching for even a tiny misdemeanour in his pupils and taking pleasure in punishing them. Some believe God is like that, wanting to send this world to hell.

But, instead, we're told God loves this world. That fact is the foundation on which everything else in Christianity is built. Paul teaches the same when he says that 'God demonstrates his love' by sending Jesus to die for sinners (Romans 5:8). God is for us, not against us. He's not out to harm. He wants to save.

2) It tells of God's act. That was to send his Son to this earth where he died in our place on the cross.

The measure of how much someone cares for you is what he'll give up for your sake. Would someone give you his seat on the bus...his last sweet...a special gift which took much of his hard-earned cash...his independence by proposing marriage...? The more he'll give up the more he cares. When God gave Jesus he gave his only Son to die. That's the measure of his love for us. There was nothing greater he could have given. He cares for us that much.

3) It tells of God's invitation. We're used to getting something only if we have the cash, the position, the relationship, or the knowledge. But eternal life cannot be bought, commanded, received as a favour, or experienced by learning alone. We can't even get it by trying to live a moral or religious life. The only way to have eternal life is to accept it as a free gift (Romans 6:23), and that free gift is for all who simply believe. Someone may never have much money, never have a position of power, never have friends in high places, never any university degrees, and never have lived a good or pious life. But he can believe. Nothing and no-one can keep him from doing that.

A minister was paying a visit to a parishioner who lived in an upstairs flat. To get there he had to enter a stairway enclosed by a glass canopy. As he went up the stairs there was a flurry of wings, a thud, and some feathers floated to the ground. A bird was trapped in the stairway, and was making furious attempts to reach freedom. Of course, it couldn't see the glass, only the blue sky. Thud! Again it threw itself against the glass. Thud! Dazed by the impact, for a moment the bird rested on the stairs. Gently the minister bent down to capture the poor creature and set it free. But as his hand came near the bird darted away. Thud! Thud! In desperation it flung itself again and again at the canopy. Once more it rested, and once more the clergyman tried to catch it only for the bird to fly away from his hand. Thud! Against the glass it went Thud! But now it fell to the stairs dead, its neck broken by the impact. The bird had struggled for a freedom it could see but not reach. The hand of love had bent down to rescue it, to give that freedom. That was its only hope, but out of fear the bird would not let itself be picked up and saved. And so it died.

God has reached down to us in Jesus to save. We must not fear him, God's gift of love, but by faith accept his grip on our lives and be made safe for all eternity.

Read also: Romans 5:6-8

10
DETERMINATION
(Philippians 3:12-14)

¹²Not that I have already obtained all this, or have already been made perfect, but I press on to take hold of that for which Christ Jesus took hold of me. ¹³Brothers, I do not consider myself yet to have taken hold of it. But one thing I do: Forgetting what is behind and straining towards what is ahead, ¹⁴I press on towards the goal to win the prize for which God has called me heavenwards in Christ Jesus.

Several words Paul uses in these verses were part of Greek athletic vocabulary. Paul probably has a scene in mind as he writes, perhaps taken from the ancient Greek games. He's picturing a runner in the final sprint for the tape, muscles bulging, lungs gasping, every sinew stretched. He's single-minded, determined, committed, keeping going even though it's hurting. He's pressing forward for the prize. If we remember that image of a runner giving his all to get to the finishing line, then we'll understand Paul's meaning in this passage. He's conscious of three things.

1) He's not yet arrived. He sees Christianity as being like a race, and no race is won on the opening lap. You must get to the finish. Paul knows he has not "already been made perfect" (verse 12). God has forgiven all his sin, but some areas of his life have still to change. Paul is saved but not yet living like his Saviour. That remains a goal. When Jesus "took hold" of Paul - his conversion on the road to Damascus - that was only the starter's pistol. It wasn't the finishing line, and he can't stop until he gets there.

2) He forgets what lies behind. A runner can neither go at speed nor in the right direction if he's facing backwards. In fact, if he's not watching where he's going he may fall or collide with an obstacle. Paul knows he can't afford to be looking over his shoulder for that would only bring back the dreadful memory of days in which he hounded Christians to death. God had forgiven that and Paul is not to dwell on it now. God has buried our sins in the depths of the sea (Micah 7:19) and put up a sign saying 'No fishing'. People with a different history to Paul's might be tempted to look back, whether to conversion itself or a time when God seemed especially close. But such clinging to the past stops them accepting the present and the future, and finding out how God wants to use them today. Those who want to win this race can't afford to be looking backwards.

3) He must press forward. No-one wins an Olympic medal without years of training and immense commitment. Running can't be his hobby; it must be his life no matter the sacrifice that involves. He has to give himself to the utmost in preparation and during the race. That's also how Paul approaches his Christianity. Every ounce of energy goes on knowing Jesus and serving him. Nothing will stop him. If the Christian race involves suffering then so be it (verses 10-11). Jesus is not his best and most important pastime; he is his life. Everything he does must help him reach the goal of heaven (verse 14). That's what he's pressing on for; that's his life's aim.

Before he was a Christian other things filled Paul's life. But now he has no time for them. The race has begun, and nothing matters more than running hard right to the end. That's the determination God expects from everyone who enters the Christian race and wants his prize.

Read also: 1 Corinthians 9:24-27

11
DO WE MATTER TO GOD?
(Isaiah 49:13-16)

13Shout for joy, O heavens;
  rejoice, O earth;
  burst into song, O mountains!
For the Lord comforts his people
  and will have compassion on his afflicted ones.

14But Zion said, "The Lord has forsaken me,
  the Lord has forgotten me."

15Can a mother forget the baby at her breast
  and have no compassion on the child she has borne?
Though she may forget,
  I will not forget you!
16See, I have engraved you on the palms of my hands;
  your walls are ever before me.

When a close relationship develops between a man and a woman, after a time one may say: "Where do we stand with each other? I must know your feelings for me." That's a tense moment. It's make or break time.

In Isaiah's day the Jewish people were asking questions about God's feelings in a similar way. What did they mean to him? Were they important? Did he care? The negative statements of verse 14 show they doubted that God was concerned about them any more. What follows is God's response in declarations of love, nowhere more profoundly and expressively than in the remarkable words, "See, I have engraved you on the palms of my hands..." Here is what that verse 16 tells us.

1) To God we are unforgettable. Verse 15 asks, 'Can a mother forget her own child?' It seems impossible, but it's not. Such a thing can and does happen. God, however, will never forget his children.

It's a common enough practice to write down a quick message on the back of your hand to remember vital information: 'Meet the wife at 11', 'See the dentist at 4', or 'Bring home a loaf of bread for tea'. Such things must not be forgotten, and so the note is written on your hand. Likewise, according to verse 16, God has our names written on his hand. He can never forget us.

But our names are not only written, they're 'engraved'. That means permanency. A ball-point pen message on your hand doesn't last. One good wash and it's gone forever. But a tattoo can't disappear. If a sailor has his sweetheart's name engraved on his arm or across his chest, that name will be with him for life. So, if God's people are engraved on the palms of God's hands their identity will be with him for ever.

When God's people question how he feels about them the answer could not be clearer: wherever we go, whatever we do, no matter how much time elapses, to God we are unforgettable.

2) To God we are unlosable. When a child is sent off to buy a bar of chocolate, Mum presses the coins into his hand and says, "Hold this tight until you get there." Perhaps for added security the money is slipped inside his glove and then he's told to hold it fast. Rattling around loose in a pocket, the money could easily be lost. Held securely in the child's hand it's safe.

And God has put us safely in the middle of his hand,

"See, I have engraved you on the palms of my hands..."
From there we're unlosable. Knowing that should bring
strength when:

Life deals hard blows. No-one would ever choose to be
out on wild seas in a terrible storm with gigantic waves.
But if someone were caught in such a storm, then the
only vessel in which he would feel safe would be an unsinkable lifeboat. Deep down most of us know that the
things we strive for in this life are all too easily sunk:
relationships, careers, money, possessions, status. But
God is unshakeable and unsinkable. If we're in his grip
we're secure.

Spiritual battles are hard. If an army's commanding
officer gives the order to advance on the enemy, infantry-
men are far more at risk than soldiers protected in a tank.
Any soldier would prefer to be surrounded by several
inches of thick steel plate rather than be out in the open
and vulnerable. Christians live in a perpetual spiritual
battle in which Satan's aim is to destroy those who have
moved from his kingdom (army) to that of God. But in
God's hand we are more protected than by any amount of
steel. When Satan tries to wrench us free, in gentle love
God simply closes his grip ever more surely round us.

All around is changing. When a family is moving from
one home to another there's hustle and bustle, packing
and unpacking, decorating and fixing, and stress and strain
for everyone. For everyone, that is, except for any little
baby in that family. The small child is picked up carefully
and lovingly in his mother's or father's arms, and carried
gently to the new home. He's not anxious. All he needs is
provided. Our world changes constantly and none of us
escape the pressure of that upheaval. Yet the hidden
reality is that we're secure in our Father's hand. There

we're watched over and safe. His hold on us is what really matters and that never changes. The strength we have is that whatever happens in our lives, we're in the palm of God's hand, and therefore unlosable to him.

3) To God we are invaluable. Take a trophy which has been engraved, run your hand over it, and you'll feel that the words or design are cut right into the glass or metal. They are not drawn on the surface, but go deep into the material.

And if we are engraved on the palms of God's hands, then our relationship with him is not superficial. Nor is it fleeting or without cost. Here is a prophetic hint that one day the nails of our sin would be engraved into and through the palms of God the Son, pinning him to a cross. What pain and suffering that must have been. He could have avoided it. Jesus could have made choices which would have led him away from Calvary. But he didn't take them. He accepted that suffering and death out of love for us.

One way of measuring love is by the amount of suffering one person will endure for the sake of another. On that basis, the evidence of God giving his Son to die at Calvary indicates supreme love. If we are worth the life of his Son, then we are truly invaluable to him.

All of this is God's doing. We matter to him. He has engraved us on the palms of his hands. Of all people, then, we must be the most secure, wanted, and loved; to him unforgettable, unlosable, invaluable.

Read also: John 10:22-30

12
AN ORDINARY SAINT
(Amos 7:12,14-16)

¹²Then Amaziah said to Amos, "Get out, you seer! Go back to the land of Judah. Earn your bread there and do your prophesying there..."
¹⁴Amos answered Amaziah, "I was neither a prophet nor a prophet's son, but I was a shepherd, and I also took care of sycamore-fig trees. ¹⁵But the Lord took me from tending the flock and said to me, 'Go, prophesy to my people Israel.' ¹⁶Now then, hear the word of the Lord..."

Amaziah has no liking for the hard message Amos is bringing. His rejection is accompanied by the comment that Amos should go elsewhere to earn his money from prophesying.

Amos responds immediately that he's no 'professional'. His origins were as a shepherd and orchard keeper (as 1:1 also mentions). But God had called him and given him words to declare to Israel. Therefore he would speak them whatever anyone said.

Here is proof that God uses ordinary people for his purposes. We imagine he's looking for 'super-saints' with special backgrounds and gifts. Significant things can be done only through them. But what kind of theology lies behind that? It's the belief that God adds his blessing to the skills of men, putting their cleverness to work for him. The Bible never teaches that. Both Old and New Testaments show that God gives gifts to ordinary people to do extra-ordinary things. Amos had no special background and no special gifts before God empowered him by the Holy Spirit.

Myra Brooks Welch penned a moving poem called *The Touch of the Master's Hand*. It's the story of an old, dusty violin being sold at auction. The auctioneer thought it hardly worth selling, and opened the bidding at only one dollar. He was pleased when it rose to three. Just as his hammer was poised to fall at that lowly sum, up to the front walked a grey-haired man. He picked up the bow, wiped the dust from the violin, tightened the strings, and began to play. The room was filled with pure and sweet music.

When he stopped, in a quiet voice the auctioneer asked once more: "What am I bidden for the old violin?" Immediately a thousand dollars was offered, then two, and finally three. Down fell the hammer, and the people cheered as the old violin was sold for three thousand dollars. But some asked what had changed the worth of the violin. Back came the answer: "The touch of the master's hand."

And the touch of the heavenly Master's hand today is still what gives value and makes a life useful. Sometimes we're written off by others; sometimes we write off ourselves. But God knows how to take mundane and hopeless people like us, touch us with his power, and use us to change his world. It's ordinary saints he uses. What God did with a shepherd and orchardkeeper like Amos he can do with us.

Read also: Matthew 4:18-22

13
FORGIVENESS: THE HARD TRUTH
(Matthew 18:21-35)

21Then Peter came to Jesus and asked, "Lord, how many times shall I forgive my brother when he sins against me? Up to seven times?"

22Jesus answered, "I tell you, not seven times, but seventy-seven times. (Or, seventy times seven)

23"Therefore, the kingdom of heaven is like a king who wanted to settle accounts with his servants. 24As he began the settlement, a man who owed him ten thousand talents was brought to him. 25Since he was not able to pay, the master ordered that he and his wife and his children and all that he had be sold to repay the debt.

26"The servant fell on his knees before him. 'Be patient with me,' he begged, 'and I will pay back everything.' 27The servant's master took pity on him, cancelled the debt and let him go.

28"But when that servant went out, he found one of his fellow-servants who owed him a hundred denarii. He grabbed him and began to choke him. 'Pay back what you owe me!' he demanded.

29"His fellow-servant fell to his knees and begged him, 'Be patient with me, and I will pay you back.'

30"But he refused. Instead, he went off and had the man thrown into prison until he could pay the debt. 31When the other servants saw what had happened, they were greatly distressed and went and told their master everything that had happened.

32"Then the master called the servant in. 'You wicked

*servant,' he said, 'I cancelled all that debt of yours because
you begged me to. ³³Shouldn't you have had mercy on your
fellow-servant just as I had on you?' ³⁴In anger his master
turned him over to the jailers to be tortured, until he should
pay back all he owed.*

*³⁵"This is how my heavenly Father will treat each of you
unless you forgive your brother from your heart."*

The sad truth about this parable, often called that of the
unmerciful servant, is that it appears here in Matthew's
gospel in order to illustrate the need for forgiveness between Christians. Jesus' story, which follows teaching on
disputes between believers, was prompted by Peter asking
about the faults of a 'brother'. Clearly even God's people
have much to learn on this subject.

The parable throws up several conclusions for us.

1) We are a people forgiven a great amount. Sometimes
we reckon our sins insignificant, that really we're fairly
lovable people, and it's only right that God should wipe out
any 'mistakes' as being perfectly excusable. When we
think like that we're like a pupil or student marking his own
exam paper, more than a little prejudiced in his own
favour. Easily he manages to overlook even serious errors
and sees good things which aren't actually there. If an
examiner marked the work a very different score would be
given.

According to this parable, our sin is like the debt of the
first servant, and that's a massive amount. Ten thousand
talents is hard to translate into today's terms, but it's a sum
which would be calculated in millions of pounds rather
than thousands. It's not surprising that Jesus says the
servant "was not able to pay" (verse 25). Instead the man
begged forgiveness, and out of pity for him the king can-

celled the whole amount (verse 27). Considering how much was owed, that is remarkable mercy.

That's the parallel to God's forgiveness of us. Our sin is also enormous, and equally we lack any means to pay for it. Our failure leaves us staring disaster in the face. And yet Jesus' death changed that. He dealt with every wrong. The Book of Hebrews is quite clear that his sacrifice was completely sufficient to remove sin (Hebrews 9:25-28).

So, the truth about our sin is that it equals the greatest debt ever owed, and we couldn't do a thing about it. But God's mercy more than matched the debt and all of it was paid by Jesus.

2) Since we are a people forgiven, in turn we must now forgive. That's precisely what the first servant didn't do. Almost his first act after receiving the king's mercy was to demand full payment from a fellow-servant who owed him a trivial sum. To be precise, a hundred denarii was one hundred thousandth of the first debt. Compared to the millions owed by the first man, this servant's debt was equivalent to the price of a modest meal. But no allowances were made this time for inability to pay and the debtor was thrown into jail.

The king was scandalised when he heard that the man whose debt he had cancelled had behaved like that. His question was, "Shouldn't you have had mercy on your fellow-servant just as I had on you?" (verse 33). That's what he would have expected to happen.

Likewise God expects that we will now forgive those who wrong us. "Forgive as the Lord forgave you," wrote Paul once (Colossians 3:13), and on another occasion he spoke of "forgiving each other, just as in Christ God forgave you" (Ephesians 4:32).

Sometimes you get to know a child, and find him noisy,

talkative, and inquisitive. After a while you realise he's simply displaying the extrovert and perceptive characteristics of his father or mother. The similar personality reveals the parentage. That's what should be happening with Christians and their heavenly Father. He forgives even massive debts against him, and therefore his children ought to display the same characteristic. That truth lies behind Paul's commands, and his Ephesian letter continues, "Be imitators of God, therefore, as dearly loved children" (Ephesians 5:1).

The parentage principle - children will have the qualities of those who gave them birth - is the basis of this story. We are expected to show the same forgiveness to others as our Father has shown to us in Christ.

3) We are not forgiven if we do not forgive. This is a hard but inescapable conclusion. Over and over the New Testament says it:

"Blessed are the merciful, for they will be shown mercy" (Matthew 5:7);

"For if you forgive men when they sin against you, your heavenly Father will also forgive you. But if you do not forgive men their sins, your Father will not forgive your sins" (Matthew 6:14-15);

"Forgive, and you will be forgiven" (Luke 6:37);

"...judgment without mercy will be shown to anyone who has not been merciful" (James 2:13).

The New Testament teaches that there will always be evidences of belonging to God. That's illustrated by talk of knowing a tree by its fruits or (as we've just noted) by the characteristics of a father being seen in his son. So, no apple tree will ever produce plums, nor will any father have a child who lacks all his features, even if only at a genetic level. Therefore if plums do appear we know the tree isn't apple by nature, or if a youngster's genetic blueprint is quite different from a particular adult we know he's not that man's child.

Here, then, is the converse of the parentage principle. The parable's message is that lack of forgiveness of others is certain evidence that a person does not have God as his Father. God's nature and God's life have not flowed into someone like that. There can be no forgiveness for him as long as that remains the case. Pardon is only for those who become children of God.

The last verse of the parable followed by its application (verses 34 and 35) leaves the terrible picture of a man who had thought he was in the clear discovering at the end that he's still liable for all his debt. So will it be for the man whose life is not changed by God, changed until even his heart is like that of his heavenly Father (verse 35).

Read also: Matthew 18:15-20

14
A QUESTION OF LIFE OR DEATH
(Deuteronomy 30:15-20)

¹⁵See, I set before you today life and prosperity, death and destruction. ¹⁶For I command you today to love the Lord your God, to walk in his ways, and to keep his commands, decrees and laws; then you will live and increase, and the Lord your God will bless you in the land you are entering to possess.

¹⁷But if your heart turns away and you are not obedient, and if you are drawn away to bow down to other gods and worship them, ¹⁸I declare to you this day that you will certainly be destroyed. You will not live long in the land you are crossing the Jordan to enter and possess.

¹⁹This day I call heaven and earth as witnesses against you that I have set before you life and death, blessings and curses. Now choose life, so that you and your children may live ²⁰and that you may love the Lord your God, listen to his voice, and hold fast to him. For the Lord is your life, and he will give you many years in the land he swore to give to your fathers, Abraham, Isaac and Jacob.

These are famous words from Scripture, addressed to the people God had rescued from captivity in Egypt. The occasion is shortly before Moses' death, just as Israel is on the edge of the Promised Land. The wilderness wanderings are over, and now God is outlining to them the possibilities for their future.

The key element here is choice. God has put before them options which will lead either to life and prosperity or to death and destruction (verse 15). If they choose to love and follow the Lord, then they will experience long life, blessing, victory over enemies, and inherit all the promises God had made to their forefathers. If they choose disobedience to God's laws, especially by worship of false gods, then they will not survive long in this new land, being overcome by other peoples.

All this is very blunt. People don't like such stark realities. We can almost imagine someone putting a counter proposition. "Let's soften this a little. We can all agree to the major rules, and to making the Lord our most important god. I'm sure he won't mind if we leave aside the lesser laws and if we give occasional attention to other, minor deities, to please the neighbours. You know, for diplomatic reasons. So, I propose we don't allow these choices today to be quite so rigid."

God's answer would be to refuse all compromise. Earlier he'd told them: "Love the Lord your God with all your heart and with all your soul and with all your strength" (Deuteronomy 6:5). Half discipleship, or even three-quarters, would never do. What is never acceptable to God is the intention to offer him less than complete devotion and obedience.

However, as God puts this stark choice to the people, what also stands out is that God wants them to choose life. He will have no pleasure in their destruction. He was their rescuer, and had brought them safely through some forty years in the wilderness. God is their Saviour, and has no wish now other than their survival and prosperity in the land he is giving to them. So, having challenged them to choose, God's heart of love is revealed: "Now choose life," he says, "so that you and your children may live..." (verse 19). How are they to do that? They'll do it by opting to love and obey the Lord. "For the Lord is your life," he continues (verse 20), and so by their allegiance to him they will inherit all the blessings he has promised.

Then, as now, people wanted happiness, peace, and their material needs met. Every generation's mistake has been to aim directly for these things. Too often they are like desert mirages, disappearing from view as soon as they seem to be reached. God's promise is that blessings are there, but only as by-products of following him. Not for a moment does that mean discipleship will produce an easy life with plenty money. Jesus gave perfect allegiance to his Father but never had much outward comfort, and following him will always involve self-sacrifice. Nevertheless, God promises blessing and provision of needs for all who will "seek first his kingdom and his righteousness" (Matthew 6:33).

God wants his people to find a fulfilled life, one with a future which runs right on to a glorious eternity. It's out of love he puts before us the blunt choice of life or death, for he wants no-one to drift off thoughtlessly into spiritual death and a lost eternity.

The film *The Champions* tells the true story of how top jockey Bob Champion battled against cancer. Chemotherapy brought him drastic side effects such as complete loss of hair and constant sickness. Week after week dragged by. He felt only weaker and weaker. His energy was gone, and his will to conquer the illness began to be sapped too.

At his lowest ebb, Bob was taken back into hospital. In depression he decided he could go on no longer, and made plans to end treatment and leave the hospital. But as he wandered around corridors in despair, he accidentally walked into the children's ward. It was full of youngsters who were also cancer victims. As he sat watching them play, a sweet little girl innocently and realistically asked him, "Are you going to live or are you going to die?" Her words burned into his mind. He paused, and then quietly but firmly replied, "I'm going to live!"

And that was the turning point. He returned to the treatment, and in time got well. He made his choice, and he lived. God also asks us to choose. On our answer to him hangs whether we will live or die for all eternity.

Read also: Romans 8:5-13

15
WHO IS OUR GOD?
(1 Kings 17:1)

Now Elijah the Tishbite, from Tishbe in Gilead, said to Ahab, "As the Lord, the God of Israel, lives, whom I serve, there will be neither dew nor rain in the next few years except at my word."

Elijah risked his life to speak to Ahab, a bad and evil king who could easily dispose of a prophet who brought an unwelcome message. It didn't pay to get on Ahab's wrong side in small things, far less to pronounce economic ruin for his country. Undaunted, Elijah gave his prophecy, and his own words reveal why.

"As the Lord...lives, whom I serve..." was his introduction. Elijah may have lived within Ahab's land, and legally Ahab was his king. But the deeper, hidden reality was that Elijah served a higher King than Ahab. He served God, and if God told him to deliver a message to Ahab then that's what he had to do. He would trust God to handle the consequences. And God did look after him, organising ravens to bring him food, and later providing equally miraculously through a penniless widow.

Elijah's actions, and the faith which went with them, showed clearly who was his real Lord. Today the same principle applies. The drum beat to which we step shows the army to which we belong. By the measure of our actions, who is our Lord? Who is our God?

Read also: John 14:15

16
TOOLS FOR A TASK
(1 Peter 4:10-11)

¹⁰Each one should use whatever gift he has received to serve others, faithfully administering God's grace in its various forms. ¹¹If anyone speaks, he should do it as one speaking the very words of God. If anyone serves, he should do it with the strength God provides, so that in all things God may be praised through Jesus Christ. To him be the glory and the power for ever and ever. Amen.

God has made his church responsible for witnessing to the lost, caring for the needy, bringing him acceptable worship, serving each other, and so on. No reasonable employer would hand out tasks without equipping the staff for the work. Has God equipped his church?

1) Each has gifts. That's the clear statement of verse 10, and there's no thought of any exceptions. No parent would give one of his children sweets, but deliberately miss another out. Why, then, do some Christians feel they have no gifts? Would the God of love forget them? All have gifts. "Each... has received ..."

Perhaps the problem for some is that they fail to notice their gifts because they don't seem very spectacular. For example, a visit to a lonely person doesn't feel like doing much for the kingdom of God compared to the work of an internationally renowned preacher. Yet any gift God has given is important. And it's needed. One small part of a 5000 piece jigsaw may not seem significant until it's missing. God gives gifts to each, because each gift is needed.

2) Each has gifts in order to serve others. The stock broker or bank manager who uses his firm's money to build himself a luxury home or to buy an expensive sports car will soon be in trouble. The money put in his care was to be used for his employer and for others, not for himself.

Similarly verse 10 says God's gifts are for others, not for personal amusement or advantage. Gifts of worship, service, and power are never to be turned inward to pep up a dull spiritual life. Besides, that doesn't work. A Christian can be strong only when he's serving God. A muscle in the body is weak unless exercised properly. Likewise real spiritual power flows through a Christian only as he uses God's gifts, and they are given for service, not self-indulgence.

3) Each has particular gifts in order to serve others. Few houses would be built, or built well, if just one tradesman was expected to be skilled at building, plumbing, joinery, plastering, and all the other jobs necessary for erecting a home. No-one is expert at everything. Neither is any Christian supposed to have every gift. That's why Peter speaks about a Christian using "whatever gift he has received".

Therefore there's no need for one Christian to feel guilty that he can't match what another does. If God hasn't given him that gift, God isn't expecting him to do that task. Equally there's no room for pride when someone does have a particularly obvious gift. Gifts are gifts, not clever skills. One person is not better than another just because God equipped him differently.

Every individual is expected to use the unique gift (or gifts) he has. To step outside the gifting of God is to wreak havoc. To do nothing with that gifting is to fail God.

4) Each has gifts in order to serve others, and in using them glorifies God. Speaking and serving is done, Peter says, "so that in all things God may be praised through Jesus Christ" (verse 11).

The great need of the world today is to hear God and experience his loving touch. Jesus is no longer on this earth in his physical form for men and women to receive his ministry. But he has a new body now - his people. When they use gifts God has given (as distinct from speaking out their own ideas or using their own methods) the authentic voice and touch of God is still heard and felt. Then people, with lives changed, will glorify God that he has met their need today.

Spiritual gifts, then, are not optional extras for those who are really keen. They are God's equipment and method so that every Christian can work for him effectively in the world today.

Read also: 1 Corinthians 12:4-11

17
GOSPEL B.C.
(Psalm 79:9-11)

⁹Help us, O God our Saviour,
for the glory of your name;
deliver us and forgive our sins
for your name's sake.
¹⁰Why should the nations say,
"Where is their God?"
Before our eyes, make known among the nations
that you avenge the outpoured blood of your servants.
May the groans of the prisoners come before you;
by the strength of your arm
preserve those condemned to die.

Some think of salvation as a New Testament idea. Certainly God's ultimate plan of how he would rescue men from their sins was fulfilled only with the coming of Jesus. But Old Testament people needed saving too, and found God just as merciful in their time. This passage shows a little of that. Verse 9 is a good example of how all the gospel elements were there in the Old Testament.

1) Admission of sin. Many try and cover up their mistakes. They don't want anyone to know what's happened, or, at least not to find out who did it. Alternatively, some hide nothing but won't accept they can be in the wrong, ever.

There is no route to salvation so long as any of these attitudes exist about sin. But in this Psalm the people are open and straight with God, admitting that they've gone wrong. Their warriors are dying in battle; enemy nations are rampaging through the land; they are without power from God; their opponents are laughing at them. All this, they know, is their own fault.

Openly they speak of 'our sins' - probably worship of false gods, injustice, and immorality. They had become like neighbouring, heathen nations. God would not tolerate such behaviour from his people and disciplined them, on this occasion by defeat in battle.

Thankfully, the result is that they accept they've been wrong. There is no denial or pretence. How can there ever be before a God who knows everything? We can hide many things from other people, but nothing from him.

2) Forgiveness for sin. These people realised they could never atone for their own sins. God had to do something to get rid of their wrongs.

Imagine that, in a fit of temper, Joe hits Fred and breaks his nose. In fact, these men are normally good friends, and this was a momentary loss of control by Joe who is almost immediately sorry. But, no matter how nice he is now to Fred, will that 'unbreak' Fred's nose? No - the damage is done, including damage to their relationship. Joe can admit he was wrong, but ultimately it's not within his power to restore the friendship. Fred, though, can choose to give forgiveness to Joe, and in that way heal their rift. He can wipe out the past wrong.

Likewise, God can give forgiveness to men. He made that possible through his Son's death on the cross. He undoes man's sin with the gift of atonement for all who believe. As these people knew so many centuries ago, no-one would save himself. God would be the "Saviour".

3) Deliverance from the effects of sin. These people needed more than the knowledge that their past wrongs were forgiven. They needed freedom from present-day invaders and murderers in their land. Their sin had left them defeated and the land wasted. So, as they plead for forgiveness, they also cry out, "Help us, O God ... deliver us."

They recognised this deliverance was also more than they could do for themselves: "...by the strength of your arm preserve those condemned to die" (verse 11). It would be God's arm that would save them. As his power came back to a forgiven people, they would be able to leave their wrong ways and begin better lives.

Christians today call that the process of sanctification. God's atonement is given immediately, but more gradually a life gets straightened out and becomes as God meant it to be. For some, that involves a significant change of morality; others must break the grip of serious drinking; a number will have to learn to forgive those who have hurt them badly in the past; yet more may need to have a fiery temper cooled or to allow patience to flourish. The Bible speaks about 'the fruit of the Spirit' and lists as examples 'peace', 'kindness', 'gentleness', 'self-control' as well as others (Galatians 5:22-23). Lives filled with that kind of fruit are what God wants, so different from what happened under the old sinful nature (Galatians 5:19-21).

An apple tree won't produce all its fruit immediately, but a healthy tree will give a good harvest eventually. Deliverance from the effects of sin - reflected in changed lives - is part of the gospel.

So, this 'gospel' is what these people looked for, and it summarises man's need today. Sin must still be confessed, forgiveness sought from God, and a new life begun. There is guaranteed success in all this for those who come honestly, helplessly, seeking. Eternal life is God's 'gift'

(Romans 6:23). We neither deserve nor earn it. What we have we owe to him. Therefore he alone deserves the praise.

Back in the times of this Psalm they knew that too, and a lovely verse outside our passage promises God his rightful glory for this forgiveness and deliverance: "Then we your people, the sheep of your pasture, will praise you for ever; from generation to generation we will recount your praise" (verse 13). We may be living many generations down the line, but we've experienced the same gospel from the same God. Therefore let the same praise be his from his people today.

Read also: Isaiah 53:3-6

18
IN THE FATHER'S HAND
(John 10:27-30)

²⁷My sheep listen to my voice; I know them, and they follow me. ²⁸I give them eternal life, and they shall never perish; no-one can snatch them out of my hand. ²⁹My Father, who has given them to me, is greater than all; no-one can snatch them out of my Father's hand. ³⁰I and the Father are one.

The words of Jesus in verse 28 that no-one can snatch his disciples from his hand give both security and protection.

Security. When a father walks down a busy street with his small son, he may say, "Come on, hold my hand." As they make their way together, the lad sees one of his school friends on the other side of the road. His reaction is to let go of Dad and dash across. But that's when he discovers that, instead of him holding on to his father's hand, in reality his father was holding on to him. He always knew the danger, and the son is held tight.

If our faith depended entirely on us, then we'd have been lost long ago. The security we have is that, even when we're weak and feel faith is failing, we don't fall out of our Father's hand because he's holding us.

Protection. Perhaps the boy's trip with his Dad is to see an important rugby match. They reach the stadium where there are thousands pressing to get in. It's all good natured, but people start pushing, and the small boy is squeezed by these huge adults around him. Suddenly he finds himself lifted up by his father's hands, high above the crowd, and placed on Dad's shoulders. Now he's safe, held up by his father's strength. And our protection as Christians lies in what God will do for us. The remarkable thought in these verses is that God takes responsibility for our well-being. Whatever the problems, doubts, or spiritual opposition, they're no match for God. Jesus said: "My Father... is greater than all" (verse 29). The pressures of life might defeat us, but never our Father.

The Christian has no guarantee of an easy life, but what encouragement there is in knowing that ultimately our security and protection are taken care of by God.

Read also: Romans 8:31-39

19
A DISPOSABLE GOD?
(Habakkuk 3:17-18)

¹⁷Though the fig-tree does not bud
*   and there are no grapes on the vines,*
though the olive crop fails
*   and the fields produce no food,*
though there are no sheep in the pen
*   and no cattle in the stalls,*
¹⁸yet I will rejoice in the Lord,
*   I will be joyful in God my Saviour.*

Some can accept God's existence only if life is going well, and nothing bad or difficult happens, especially to them. They believe in God as long as they have comfort and happiness. But if they experience sadness or poverty, they say, "There can't be a God or he wouldn't allow these things to happen." Others tend the same way but stop one point short. They retain a belief in God's existence, but see him as harsh, uncaring, and remote. There's little incentive for them to worship such a God.

Habakkuk fits neither of these categories. His God not only existed, but was always one of love and goodness, deserving to receive joyful praise. Why?

1) His belief was not determined by circumstances. God's existence and character were objective realities, not matters decided by the events of Habakkuk's life. God was not alive and kind only when Habakkuk's circumstances were easy, any more than he was dead or bad when those circumstances were difficult. Habakkuk knew God was

God whether he prospered or went hungry.

For people of his day, the lack of a harvest was a serious thing. But such a lack didn't mean God had fallen out of heaven, nor that he didn't care. There were plenty other reasons for crop failure, anything from the use of poor agricultural methods to God's loving discipline of his people for their sin. Failure might prompt many questions, but none of them need doubt God.

2) His God deserved worship whatever the circumstances. It's not right to be interested in someone only when you stand to gain. Perhaps you hope he will buy you a meal, or give you a gift. But is that friendship? Or is it a subtle form of exploitation? Habakkuk couldn't worship God like that. His praise and rejoicing in God could not depend on getting a successful harvest from him. The experiences of life did not determine his relationship with God. He rejoices in God because he is the Lord. God made him and rules over him. Therefore he deserves to be honoured.

Habakkuk also recognises God as his Saviour. His life would be nothing without God's mercy. He has needed his sins forgiven, rescue from enemies, and to be given hope beyond death. None of these he could achieve himself, but God has provided them. Such a Saviour deserves to be thanked and worshipped.

We live in a society which disposes of anything inconvenient or redundant. If something gives us no positive 'return' we get rid of it. Many have brought that attitude to the matter of faith, and have 'disposed' of God when he didn't provide everything they wanted. Habakkuk learned to rejoice in his living and loving God no matter the outward circumstances. We would do well to learn from him.

Read also: Philippians 4:11-13

20
FAITH - LIVING DANGEROUSLY
(Acts 3:1-10)

¹One day Peter and John were going up to the temple at the time of prayer - at three in the afternoon. ²Now a man crippled from birth was being carried to the temple gate called Beautiful, where he was put every day to beg from those going into the temple courts. ³When he saw Peter and John about to enter, he asked them for money. ⁴Peter looked straight at him, as did John. Then Peter said, "Look at us!" ⁵So the man gave them his attention, expecting to get something from them.

⁶Then Peter said, "Silver or gold I do not have, but what I have I give you. In the name of Jesus Christ of Nazareth, walk." ⁷Taking him by the right hand, he helped him up, and instantly the man's feet and ankles became strong. ⁸He jumped to his feet and began to walk. Then he went with them into the temple courts, walking and jumping, and praising God. ⁹When all the people saw him walking and praising God, ¹⁰they recognised him as the same man who used to sit begging at the temple gate called Beautiful, and they were filled with wonder and amazement at what had happened to him.

As Christians we say we live by faith and not by sight (2 Corinthians 5:7), but actually we like to reverse these. We prefer to have the future guaranteed to succeed before we'll go forward: in some financial matter; in a career; into a relationship; in planning for our church or some other organisation. This story shows that having faith is never like that. Instead it always seems to involve risk.

1) The risks of failure were considerable. This man had been disabled from birth, and people carried him every day to beg beside the entrance to the temple (verse 2). His prominent location, and perhaps his life-long and severe handicap, had made him famous. Later on, after the healing, the man and his changed condition were immediately recognised. Everyone knew him, and knew what he did. What he did, of course, was beg for money. So, when Peter and John came by, that's all he was looking for from them (verse 3). If ever there was a 'hard' case for healing, in terms of high public profile, serious condition, and low expectation, this was it. The risks of ministering to him were considerable. Ridicule and humiliation were certain consequences of failure.

2) A step of faith was inevitable. There was no rise of faith in the man. Verse 5 shows that even when he gave Peter and John full attention it was only because he expected money. Nor was there the context of a prayer meeting or worshipping congregation to give the apostles' faith some wings. But they knew Jesus had healed the sick and had promised to keep doing that through them. So, with nothing else to offer the man, they took the risk of faith and committed themselves in trust that God would act: "...what I have I give you. In the name of Jesus Christ of Nazareth, walk." (verse 6)

Then they helped him up, and as they did his feet and ankles were made strong. He was healed, and ran and jumped through the whole temple area attracting a huge crowd to whom Peter and John were able eventually to tell the gospel.

But notice the miracle happened only after the step of faith. They had to speak out and reach out to the man first. That was quite a step. If they promised healing and the man stayed lame their reputation would be buried there and then. They knew that. Yet, to have been put off by that thought, to have held back in fear, would have left a man crippled and begging for the rest of his life. Rather than that, they risked all, and he was healed.

To do anything without guaranteed results is always risky, and therefore there's only spiritual paralysis for Christians who are looking for a safe life.

Two keys to minimising risk are implied here and are relevant to anything we do.

a) *Know the power of God.* The apostles had seen Jesus heal cripples before, and countless other people with serious and long-term illnesses. They knew what God could do. In themselves, they had nothing to offer this man. But God did. His condition was well within God's capabilities to change. Therefore they could trust him. Likewise, the more we know our God the more we'll believe he can change what seems impossible.

b) *Know what he commands you to do.* Healing this beggar fitted with Christ's commission to these men. Jesus had healed many, and authorised his disciples to continue that work (Matthew 10:1,8; 28:20). So, that day at the Temple, the apostles weren't indulging their own fantasies; they were carrying out orders. Every believer has God's power, but there's no licence with it for use anywhere we want. Power is given to do God's will. Again it's living close to God that brings knowledge of his will, and with that a sense of safety in attempting what others would think ridiculous. Living by faith always includes living with risk. But knowing the power and will of God minimises fear and weakness and maximises joy and effectiveness in serving him.

Read also: Exodus 14:10-31

21
JESUS EVICTED
(Revelation 3:19-22)

[19]"Those whom I love I rebuke and discipline. So be earnest, and repent. [20]Here I am! I stand at the door and knock. If anyone hears my voice and opens the door, I will come in and eat with him, and he with me.

[21]To him who overcomes, I will give the right to sit with me on my throne, just as I overcame and sat down with my Father on his throne. [22]He who has an ear, let him hear what the Spirit says to the churches."

From heaven Jesus is speaking to the church at Laodicea. Already his words to them had been tough regarding their lukewarmness (verse 16). Now, in verse 20, comes a scenario depicting both failure and opportunity. It's portrayed to them in terms of Jesus coming to their door.

1) Christ is outside. That's where he begins. "Of course," someone might say, "Where else could he be at this point in the story?" The answer is that already he could and should be on the inside. Jesus is standing outside his own house. These words are not spoken to unbelievers, but to members of a Christian church. At least that's what they were in name, and if they're Christians Jesus ought to be right in the midst of them. That's where he belongs. But he's not. He's been shut out. What makes that even more tragic is that until now they hadn't noticed his absence. They'd been getting on with their lives, and hadn't even realised Jesus wasn't there.

2) Christ wants entry. "I stand at the door and knock,"

he says. Though they've ignored him, left him outside, he hasn't stormed off, abandoning them. He wants to be in the middle of those who call themselves Christians.

But he isn't making a forced entry. He isn't beating down the door. He won't make them honour him as Lord. Love never bullies anyone. It won't even compel an unwilling person into heaven. But it does invite, and here is the King of the universe, humbly and patiently knocking. He wants these people to choose to let him in.

3) Christ promises to enter. He isn't teasing. He isn't like a mischievous child who rings a doorbell and then hides or runs away when someone answers. Rather, if they will hear his knock and open the door, Jesus will definitely and immediately come in. What's more, he'll stay. A meal in ancient times was unhurried. It was the time of fellowship. Jesus' promise to enter and eat is a way of saying he will share life with the person who makes him welcome.

So, by potent imagery, Christ shows a church its fault and its opportunity to put the fault right. That's love. He does not leave people complacent in their sin; neither does he only criticise. He shows them how they can still be saved.

To people today the same invitation to fellowship is there. Jesus may well have been left on the outside, even by those who say they believe. Perhaps they attend church, perhaps pray, perhaps read their Bibles. But these things are done more from habit than intimacy; there is no personal fellowship with Jesus. Before such people the living, reigning Christ stands and knocks. Though they've hurt him, back he comes in love.

For those who have known nothing other than a formal belief in a remote Christ, here is the opportunity of deep and lasting fellowship with the Saviour of men.

Read also: John 6:35-40

22
PRAYER WORKS
(2 Chronicles 20:12)

"O our God, will you not judge them? For we have no power to face this vast army that is attacking us. We do not know what to do, but our eyes are upon you."

Jehoshaphat, king of Judah, ended his prayer with these words as his people faced potential annihilation at the hands of a massive invasion force of Moabites, Ammonites, and some Meunites (verse 1). His prayer was answered in a powerful yet surprising way, as God caused the invaders to turn on each other. Judah marched out praising God and found no army to face, only dead bodies strewn everywhere (verse 24). If ever there was a 'successful' prayer it was this one. Two features especially made it so.

1) Acceptance of personal weakness. Jehoshaphat was in no doubt what Judah's chances were on their own. They were significantly outnumbered by this combined force, and facing certain defeat: "...we have no power to face this vast army that is attacking us."

Jehoshaphat was exactly right. They had no power. But that admission of weakness with the subsequent appeal for help showed their belief that God did have power. Why else would they pray to him? If you're in debt and needing financial rescue, you don't ask a friend who is as bankrupt as you. You look around for someone who is well-off and plead your cause with him.

So these people had a 'hands-off' approach. The situation was beyond them. Only God could save them now. They were admitting their weakness, and asking for his strength.

That's how it must be with prayer. People learning to drive a car are sometimes taught in a vehicle with dual controls. That way, if the learner gets into difficulty, the instructor can take over. What spells disaster, though, is if the pupil still tries to drive when the instructor should have control. One mustn't accelerate while the other is braking. Both can't drive simultaneously. Either the teacher or the pupil is in control, but never both.

Likewise, either we are in control of our lives or God is. Both can't be. We need to let God take charge by admitting our inability to handle situations. Then we're not interfering, not still trying to run our lives our own way.

2) Looking for God's answer. Jehoshaphat and his people had to admit to God that they hadn't a single solution to their problem. They confessed that any answer would have to come from God. Their faith was utterly in him: "We do not know what to do, but our eyes are upon you."

What a refreshing change this is from so many prayers. Often we don't pray requests to God. We pray answers. We've made up our minds in advance what we would like to happen, and we instruct God in prayer that that's what he should do. Of course we make it sound spiritual, and we tell God we're trusting him for such-and-such to happen. There, we've had faith. That must be a good thing.

But it isn't good if in reality we've been ordering God about. What a futile exercise that is. He is the Lord, not us. He will not be told what to do, and all we achieve by our narrow, blinkered approach is that we miss God's answer.

No-one could have accused Jehoshaphat and company

of simply seeking God's blessing on their plan. Indeed, none of them would ever have been so crazy as to propose a strategy which sent them marching out to face their foe doing nothing other than praising God. Probably their strategy - if they'd had one - would have involved ambushes or attempts to divide the invaders. If they'd offered nominal prayers for divine approval of that idea, and then gone ahead with it, the corpses in the desert would have been theirs.

Thankfully they didn't dictate any solution to God. They put their lives into his hands, and looked for his way forward. They were open to his will, whatever it was. When they obeyed what he said they experienced a result more dramatic and decisive than anything they could have dared to pray for. Their victory was complete.

God is more than able to deal with our problems. Of course prayers of faith are right, but they must never be twisted into attempts to manipulate God to do what we want. That will never work.

Stage one of intercessory prayer is the acceptance of our weakness. Stage two is looking for God's answer.

Once we master both of these, we may find our prayers are being answered differently from how we expect. But we'll be in no doubt that they're being answered. And perhaps some of those answers will be victories as surprising but as necessary as that experienced by Jehoshaphat and the people of Judah.

Read also: 2 Corinthians 1:8-11

23
KNOWN BY GOD
(Isaiah 44:24)

"This is what the Lord says - your Redeemer, who formed you in the womb..."

We're influenced by many people, perhaps most by relatives. For example, what parents say carries great weight because we want to please them. Friends, neighbours, colleagues at work - our peer groups - also make a great difference to what we do. Advertisers and fashion designers affect us. So do the statements of politicians, even taking into account our scepticism. There are so many voices, so many influences.

God's appeal is that we should listen to him above all others. He is the Lord, so he is ruler over all the earth, including our lives. He is our Redeemer, rescuing us from sin and giving a new future. We owe everything to him. Clearly we should listen to the One who is both Lord and Redeemer.

"And" - God says - "I am the one who formed you in the womb." That's a statement worth remembering when issues concerning the value of an unborn child are being discussed. But God's point here is that he both made us and knows us. Even in the biological sense we owe our lives to him. So from our earliest days he's understood us, and led us through life step by step to where we are now. No-one knows us like our God.

Clearly no-one, then, can direct us with authority and sureness like our God. As Lord he has the right and as

Maker he has the knowledge to guide us. Before we listen to any other voice, let's listen to God. Supremely we are known by him, and he wants us to heed what he says.

Read also: John 10:1-10

24
BRINGING UP JUNIOR
(Psalm 127)

¹Unless the Lord builds the house,
*   its builders labour in vain.*
Unless the Lord watches over the city,
*   the watchmen stand guard in vain.*
²In vain you rise early
*   and stay up late,*
toiling for food to eat -
*   for he grants sleep to those he loves.*
³Sons are a heritage from the Lord,
*   children a reward from him.*
⁴Like arrows in the hands of a warrior
*   are sons born in one's youth.*
⁵Blessed is the man
*   whose quiver is full of them.*
They will not be put to shame
*   when they contend with their enemies in the gate.*

Some parents will have a wry smile that the same Psalm which speaks so much about children also promises sleep. Perhaps that's the nearest we'll ever come to finding a contradiction within Scripture!

The second half of the Psalm is all about children. Because Jewish society (like all ancient civilizations) valued male offspring over female, sons are featured although the truths apply equally to daughters.

The central idea here is that children are a 'heritage' from the Lord. If that is so, several things follow.

1) Children belong to the Lord and not to their parents.
That would have been a revolutionary idea to the Romans and Greeks of old. They regarded children as objects owned by their parents who had full rights of disposal over them. A father could sell his children as slaves, punish them in any way he liked even with the death penalty, or simply abandon them. Unwanted children were left in Rome's Forum where they became the property of anyone who picked them up. Frail children were often not allowed to live. The Stoic Seneca wrote of how mad or sick animals were slaughtered and while he was on the subject added, "Children who are born weakly and deformed we drown." His attitude, as that of most people of his time, was that a child belonged to parents who could do with 'it' as they pleased.

Today society's values are thankfully different, although some basic attitudes haven't changed. Anyone who tries to tell a mother how to bring up her child will soon be informed, "Mind your own business. I'll bring up my child my way!"

The Christian view of children is that fundamentally they are God's, not ours: 'a heritage from the Lord'. That certainly prohibits throwing them out, but it also means we can't raise them just as we please.

Over-discipline or lack of discipline are equally unacceptable. They must be taught all they need to know, but without such a concentration on intellectual knowledge that they fail to develop all-round personalities and social skills. Nor dare they be brought up either undernourished or overfed. These children belong to God and he expects them to be looked after properly.

If someone borrows a friend's brand new car he takes extra-special care of it. Nothing dare go wrong. Knowing how much it matters to its owner, he must hand it back in perfect condition. Something similar should be our attitude with regard to how we treat our children. They are to be returned to God in a 'condition' which pleases him.

2) The responsibility of parenthood is from the Lord. This Psalm speaks about heritage. That's a word we hear today in many contexts. It might concern our architectural heritage, the grandeur of old buildings, or our intellectual heritage, referring to the thoughts and writings of great philosophers. It could mean our literary heritage of great classics, or our artistic heritage of paintings.

One idea is common to all these uses of the same word: something of importance has been left to the present generation for which it must assume responsibility. That's why people speak of guarding or restoring our heritage. An object, skill, or tradition of value has been handed on to us and we must care for it.

That principle forms part of the teaching here about children. They are given to us on the understanding that we accept responsibility and look after them on God's behalf. No-one dare treat children, then, as a nuisance or hobby. No-one can be cruel or thoughtless toward them. Each child will need adequate love, time and care. Each will also cost money, though expensive gifts must never become a substitute for the attention they require.

If children are a heritage given by God, then parenthood is a serious responsibility.

3) Accountability for what we do with our children is to the Lord. As mentioned earlier, no-one would lend out his valuable car and then forget about it, or take no interest in its condition when it was returned. Likewise God holds parents answerable for what we do with his children. How we've treated them, the example we've set, the teaching we've given, and the guidance on which they've based decisions...all of that is important to him.

The task of parenthood is to take a completely dependent and helpless baby and through some 18 or 20 years transform that child into an independent and competent adult. How well we do that matters to God. Romans 14:12 says, "So then, each of us will give an account of himself to God." There are no areas exempt from that divine audit. We will answer to God for how we have raised the children for whom he's made us responsible.

If this role of parenthood is that serious, we'd better be sure our guidance, inspiration, and strength are coming from God for the task. Our own abilities will not be enough. Thankfully God's resources are never in short supply. "If any of you lacks wisdom, he should ask God, who gives generously to all without finding fault, and it will be given to him" (James 1:5). God's storehouse of all necessary qualities is there to be used by us for the work of parenthood because he wants us to succeed. He wants that for our sakes, and also for the sake of the children that he has given us in this world.

Read also: Ephesians 6:1-4

25
WHAT'S IN A NAME?
(Matthew 1:20-21)

²⁰But after he had considered this, an angel of the Lord appeared to him in a dream and said, "Joseph son of David, do not be afraid to take Mary home as your wife, because what is conceived in her is from the Holy Spirit. ²¹She will give birth to a son, and you are to give him the name Jesus, because he will save his people from their sins."

Names like Barber, Smith, Taylor, or Hunter often show the kind of work done by people's distant ancestors. In centuries gone by, names were descriptions, not titles. It was the same in Israel of old. A name summed up someone's character or described his purpose in life.

When Joseph is told to accept Mary as his wife, he's also given instructions on how to name the child she will bear: "...you are to give him the name Jesus" (verse 21). Jesus is the Greek form of the Hebrew Joshua, and it means 'Yahweh (Jehovah) is salvation'. The angel brings out that emphasis when he adds, "because he will save his people from their sins."

With that name and angelic explanation, then, what are we being told about this baby?

Firstly, we're being told that this is no ordinary child. Mary and Joseph will be thought of as his parents, but his real Father is God since he has been conceived by the Holy Spirit (verse 20).

In fact, the words used point powerfully to the oneness of Father and Son. The name means that God saves while the work Jesus will do is to save. That's not similar activity by two different individuals. It's the same activity by the same God, Father and Son.

That conjunction may be what triggered Matthew to think of Isaiah's prophecy of the virgin conceiving a child who would have the name 'Immanuel' which means 'God with us' (verse 23 quoting Isaiah 7:14). God will have come among men in a child who bears his name.

Clearly, secondly, there's a significant statement being made about his purpose. Jesus is coming to "save his people from their sins."

The baby would grow to be a man who one day would set his face towards Jerusalem, knowing that city would have a cross on which he would hang. He would accept that suffering deliberately, because "the Son of Man did not come to be served, but to serve, and to give his life as a ransom for many" (Matthew 20:28). His death on the cross would save many.

So here is probably the only child ever born with the purpose of dying.

That's why any Christmas message which forgets Easter is devalued. Christmas certainly isn't about presents, trees and tinsel. But neither is it only about a beautiful story of the birth of a special baby. If we stop with that we have little more than spiritualised sentimentality. The angel told Joseph from the beginning that this child came with a mission to save men. That was fulfilled only when he suffered and died at Calvary.

'Yahweh is salvation' was his name. It was a significant name, given to a child who was also God, and who would lay down his life to save us.

Read also: Luke 1:26-38

26
THE CHURCH: WHAT GOD WANTS
(Acts 2:42-47)

42They devoted themselves to the apostles' teaching and to the fellowship, to the breaking of bread and to prayer. 43Everyone was filled with awe, and many wonders and miraculous signs were done by the apostles. 44All the believers were together and had everything in common. 45Selling their possessions and goods, they gave to anyone as he had need. 46Every day they continued to meet together in the temple courts. They broke bread in their homes and ate together with glad and sincere hearts, 47praising God and enjoying the favour of all the people. And the Lord added to their number daily those who were being saved.

The church consists of people gathered by God for God. It's his church. What, then, does God require of his people?

1) He requires them to grow up. Those who already have children are usually aware that any addition to the family will be both a blessing and a burden. As well as bringing joy, the new arrival will take the parents back to sleepless nights, frayed nerves, and a chaotic home. That's bad enough. Imagine how much worse if the other children had never grown up. If they were still babies, and making those demands too, the parents would go completely demented!

God means for those 'born again' of the Spirit to grow up, and not remain baby Christians. That's why these disciples 'devoted themselves to the apostles' teaching' (verse 42). The early converts didn't know what Jesus had said and done, but the apostles did. Therefore they could learn from them.

Besides, their greatest desire was to find out more about Jesus. When people are keen about a hobby or sport they read every book on the subject, attend classes, practice feverishly, and fire a thousand questions at anyone who may know more than they do. Christians will grow up in their faith when they apply that kind of determination to learning about their Saviour and Lord.

2) He requires them to grow together. When a child is born into an existing family he doesn't acquire only parents but also brothers and sisters. They come as part of the package of life and he has to learn to get on with them. Likewise no-one can be a Christian alone. As well as a heavenly Father there's a ready made family to which he belongs automatically and to whom he must relate.

Because of that the first Christians "devoted them-selves... to the fellowship" (verse 42), "had everything in common", "gave to anyone as he had need" (verses 44-45), and met every day to worship and share meals (verse 46). They were all joined to the one Jesus, and therefore were intimately and unavoidably linked to each other too. A tree is alive when the sap flows out to every extremity. It's dead when that stops. Perhaps it still stands, but no longer do its roots suck life into the trunk and out to leaves. In time it must fall. The source of life is gone. That and only that held the tree together. Likewise, a church is alive only when Christ's life flows through its members. If that life stops flowing between them then, no matter how impres-sive the parts, what remains is only the dead outward form of a church.

Such fellowship doesn't happen by accident any more

than good family life comes without effort. It requires time for each other, loving attitudes, readiness to forgive, and willingness to serve. Those are all fundamental characteristics, fitting with the fruit the Holy Spirit wants to grow in his people: love, joy, peace, patience, kindness, goodness, faithfulness, gentleness and self-control (Galatians 5:22-23). All of these are qualities needed for good relationships. No-one is on a private pilgrimage to heaven. God requires fellowship between fellow-travellers.

3) He requires them to grow out. God has no intention of having a small family! He wants the numbers to grow. As these early believers shared their common life and worship, and told of their faith, "the Lord added to their number daily those who were being saved" (verse 47).

No Christian can change the evil of men who refuse to believe. But we can do something about the ignorance of men who have never had the chance to believe. Many think Christianity is only a message of 'do your best and say your prayers', and have no realisation that it is good news of forgiveness for those who will admit they've failed a holy God. God wants all men to hear that, and every member of God's family has the responsibility to tell it.

But some prefer to leave that task to the minister or pastor. "It's his job," they say. It is, but not only his. The Bible teaches that it's everyone's job. Jesus said: "Go into all the world and preach the good news to all creation" (Mark 16:15). There's no suggestion that only some should do that. In any case, as someone has put it, "It's not the shepherd who begets the sheep. Sheep beget sheep."

Sharing the faith can seem frightening and difficult, but really it's no more than telling what you know to be true. Someone who was seriously ill but then operated on and cured by a top surgeon won't hesitate to tell of his experience if he meets someone else with the same medical condition. He might not understand every detail of his disease or its cure, but he's glad to let the other person know where to go for treatment. Witnessing about Jesus is no different in principle from that. We've been cured from sin, and we tell others where to find the same healing from that fatal disease. It's the job of every Christian because God requires his family to grow out.

Sadly, some say they are put off the Christian faith because of the church. They don't want to become like the Christians they see. Growing up, growing together, and growing out would make us more like the attractive people of God which these first Christians clearly were, "enjoying the favour of all the people" (verse 47).

Read also: Ephesians 4:1-6; 11-16

27
PRAISE THE LORD
(Psalm 117)

¹Praise the Lord, all you nations;
extol him, all you peoples.
²For great is his love towards us
and the faithfulness of the Lord endures for ever.
Praise the Lord.

This is the shortest Psalm; indeed, it is the shortest individual section of Scripture. Yet its brevity robs it of nothing in richness. It teaches:

1) The Lord is to be praised. The Psalm opens and closes with that instruction. The Hebrew phrase for 'Praise the Lord' is 'Hallelu Yah'. Every time we say that, we're proclaiming praise to God. Rightly so. The earth revolves around the sun, and from it draws heat, light, and energy, and could not exist otherwise. Likewise man draws his blessings from God, his Maker, and would be and have nothing without him. Therefore God should be praised.

2) The Lord is to be praised by all. The command to praise goes to "all you nations" and "all you peoples". The God who made all should be praised by all. Neither Israel of old nor Christians today can 'own' God and keep him as their private possession. All men must be given the opportunity to know and worship him.

3) The Lord is to be praised for his great love and faithfulness. Clearly this Creator is not aloof from those he has made. Even though they've gone far wrong he has not washed his hands of them. Instead, says the Psalmist, he shows love and faithfulness. Love is his very nature (1 John 4:8), and so every act of his is loving. That nature is unchanging (James 1:17), and therefore he's consistent in all he does.

Those who know a God who is always good to his people must surely proclaim Hallelu Yah, Praise the Lord.

Read also: Psalm 150

28
ESCAPING GOD'S WRATH
(Romans 1:18-20)

[18]The wrath of God is being revealed from heaven against all the godlessness and wickedness of men who suppress the truth by their wickedness, [19]since what may be known about God is plain to them, because God has made it plain to them. [20]For since the creation of the world God's invisible qualities - his eternal power and divine nature - have been clearly seen, being understood from what has been made, so that men are without excuse.

This passage introduces a catalogue of evil behaviour, everything from the worship of images to perverted sexual practices. What's remarkable is not that man does such things, but that he does them in defiance of the truth he knows about God.

Paul points out that from the very beginning of time the essential facts about God have been obvious from the world he created. We know that a beautiful and sensitive picture must have been painted by a skilful and thoughtful artist. A complex and efficient piece of machinery must have been designed by an intelligent and painstaking engineer. Anything that is made carries a message about its maker. The same is true with our world. God's handiwork there tells us about him.

Had that not been so, then men might never have known there was a God. Or, had the world been made a place of darkness or disorder, men might have thought him to be aging, feeble or insignificant. But, says Paul, the presence of a carefully ordered creation not only indicates that God exists but also that he has eternal power and a divine nature. To ignore such a God as this, then, and enter into disobedient and evil behaviour, is to suppress the truth deliberately, leaving men without excuse.

A motorist is cruising towards town at 50 m.p.h. As he approaches a 30 m.p.h. speed limit sign he glances in his mirror, and sees a police car on his tail. If at that moment he accelerates he's acting in clear defiance of the authorities. He can have no excuse when he's pulled over and booked. Mankind - choosing to do wrong while knowing of God - is equally without excuse, and must face the penalty.

That penalty is severe. God does not turn a blind eye to man's evil. Nor is this God of eternal power unable to deal with man. In fact his wrath is already being experienced as men sink into an ever deeper morass of trouble (Romans 1:26-32). Horrendous though that is, it can be only the beginning. Paul speaks later of "the day of God's wrath, when his righteous judgment will be revealed" (Romans 2:5).

If the misery and darkness of our world now is no more than a foretaste of God's anger against man, then no-one of any sense will continue to live against God and experience that complete and final judgment. Instead that person will immediately embrace God's only but powerful way of saving man, the gospel of Jesus Christ (Romans 1:16).

Read also: Hebrews 4:12-16

29
MISSION IMPOSSIBLE
(Judges 6:14-16)

¹⁴The Lord turned to him and said, "Go in the strength you have and save Israel out of Midian's hand. Am I not sending you?"

¹⁵"But Lord," Gideon asked, "how can I save Israel? My clan is the weakest in Manasseh, and I am the least in my family."

¹⁶The Lord answered, "I will be with you, and you will strike down all the Midianites together."

Poor Gideon! Not for one moment did he want the job of leading the opposition to an invading army so numerous it could be likened only to swarms of locusts (verse 5). Most Israelites were hiding among the mountains (verse 2), and Gideon would have been much happier to stay there himself, threshing his wheat in a winepress in order not to be noticed. Besides, he couldn't exactly boast a fighting pedigree, hastily pointing out to God that his clan was the weakest in Manasseh, and he was the least significant in his clan (verse 15).

Nevertheless, he was God's man to rout the Midianites, and two factors appear here which should have encouraged him to believe he could do the impossible.

1) God's commission. "Am I not sending you?" God asked the reluctant Gideon. The plan to use him was God's idea, not his. If this young man had merely had some crazy notion of his own to be Israel's liberator, his ambitions and his men would have died under the swords of a strong enemy. But the result would be very different if God was sending him. No matter how many Midianite soldiers there were, God would give success.

Centuries later the early Christians began the seemingly impossible task of evangelising a hostile world. Almost immediately they were persecuted, and the Jewish Sanhedrin had the apostles thrown into jail. Some of the elders of the Sanhedrin were so incensed they wanted to execute these men who accused them of crucifying God's Saviour. But one Pharisee, Gamaliel, told them: "Leave these men alone! Let them go! For if their purpose or activity is of human origin, it will fail. But if it is from God, you will not be able to stop these men; you will only find yourselves fighting against God" (Acts 5:38-39).

That wise teacher of Israel was right. When God is behind something it succeeds, and no-one can oppose it. Those, therefore, who have God's commission can go forward with confidence no matter how daunting their work seems.

2) God's company. When Gideon pleaded his own weakness, God's firm reply was: "I will be with you, and you will strike down all the Midianites together." Alone Gideon didn't stand a chance. With God alongside, it would be the Midianites who would be destroyed. His company would make all the difference. The presence and power of God, not Gideon's strength or tactics, would win this fight.

Filled more with enthusiasm than ability, a man joined a choir. While not quite useless, he found himself frequently singing notes different from anyone else. His unique part was not appreciated by his fellows. One large, broad-chested bass standing behind our tuneless friend, whispered a solution. "When we begin, lean back against me." The advice seemed strange, but the newcomer was more than aware by now of his inability and willing to try anything. The organ began to play, the choir sang, and the man leaned back against the strong singer's chest. Immediately he felt the deep resonance of the bass singer's voice, and to his amazement found his own voice begin to harmonize with the other choirman's notes. As long as he leaned against his fellow, that man's musical ability coursed through him, and a new power and quality of singing emerged.

Gideon was being given the opportunity to lean on God so his power would flow through him to do this work. Without God it was impossible. With him the Midianites would be routed.

God's presence is guaranteed also to all who are carrying out his commission today. None of us are abandoned to our tasks. We are not alone. God's company follows his commission, and thus impossible tasks are done.

Read also: Matthew 28:18-20

30
EASTER'S "B" SIDE
(1 Corinthians 15:12-23)

[12]But if it is preached that Christ has been raised from the dead, how can some of you say that there is no resurrection of the dead? [13]If there is no resurrection of the dead, then not even Christ has been raised. [14]And if Christ has not been raised, our preaching is useless and so is your faith. [15]More than that, we are then found to be false witnesses about God, for we have testified about God that he raised Christ from the dead. But he did not raise him if in fact the dead are not raised. [16]For if the dead are not raised, then Christ has not been raised either. [17]And if Christ has not been raised, your faith is futile; you are still in your sins. [18]Then those also who have fallen asleep in Christ are lost. [19]If only for this life we have hope in Christ, we are to be pitied more than all men.

[20]But Christ has indeed been raised from the dead, the firstfruits of those who have fallen asleep. [21]For since death came through a man, the resurrection of the dead comes also through a man. [22]For as in Adam all die, so in Christ all will be made alive. [23]But each in his own turn: Christ, the firstfruits; then, when he comes, those who belong to him.

When pop musicians bring out a 'single' it usually has an 'A' side and a 'B' side. The 'A' side has the song the artist means the disc jockeys to play, the one he hopes will get to number one in the charts. The 'B' side is little more than a fill-in. Sometimes a singer comes up with two equally good songs with neither intended to be more important than the other. Both are meant to be heard and appreciated.

Easter is like that second situation. Some might think all that really matters is Jesus' death on the cross, with the forgiveness of sins it brings. That's their 'A' side, with the resurrection little more than a happy ending to the story, a 'B' side fill-in. But the Bible always shows the resurrection as equally significant.

It was the main theme of Peter's first sermon on the Day of Pentecost (Acts 2), and still at the forefront of his mind when he penned his epistle. There he wrote that God "has given us new birth into a living hope through the resurrection of Jesus Christ from the dead" (1 Peter 1:3). The resurrection was at the centre of the controversy Paul stirred up in Athens: "Paul was preaching the good news about Jesus and the resurrection" (Acts 17:18). And it's that topic which occupies almost this whole chapter of the apostle's letter to the Corinthians. These writers believed the resurrection belonged with the cross. Neither was dispensable.

One of the reasons for the significance of the resurrection is that it is proof.

1) It is proof that Jesus was who he said he was. Anyone can claim to be the Saviour of men. The world is littered with self- appointed gurus and prophets, and every psychiatric hospital has its share of patients suffering delusions. Words are cheap, and alone are never enough. A salesman who claims record sales with his last company will be expected to deliver a full order book in this job too. If he can't, his words don't impress any more. In any sphere, we must fulfil what we say; if we can't, people write us off.

Jesus said he could forgive sins (Mark 2:10), give men life to the full (John 10:10), and that he and God the Father were one (John 10:30). He accepted Peter's recognition of him as the Messiah, the Son of God (Matthew 16:16-17).

He told his disciples to trust in him as they did in God, that he would prepare a place for them in heaven, that they could get to God only through him, and that they must obey what he commanded (John 14:1,2,6,15). He also said he would die as a ransom for others, but be raised to life on the third day (Matthew 20:28; 16:21). These are the kind of claims Jesus made. They could be no more than the ravings of a lunatic. Evidence to substantiate them is needed if they are to be taken seriously.

That's what the resurrection is. No-one ever rose from the dead just because he said he would. The power of God - and only the power of God - can bring someone back from the grave. So, the fact that Jesus' statement that he would rise from death was fulfilled becomes strong evidence that Jesus was neither a boaster nor a lunatic. And, if he can be right about overcoming death, then it puts all his words on a new footing. He said he was the Son of God. Because of the resurrection we must take that seriously. Jesus has proved himself.

2) It is proof that sin's power is broken. In 1 Corinthians 15:12-19, Paul shows what follows if there is no resurrection from the dead. It would mean Jesus had not been raised either, and that would annul the whole Christian faith. He concludes: "...if Christ has not been raised, your faith is futile; you are still in your sins" (verse 17). In other words, what hope has man if Jesus hasn't overcome death?

His reasoning is this. It is sin which leads to death, and no-one before had ever beaten that great enemy. (Even those Jesus had brought back to life would die again.) No-one had ever gone through death to a new and eternal life. Suppose no-one could? World War II finally ended because an atom bomb was dropped on Hiroshima. One weapon of that magnitude nullified all the conventional forces and armaments which Japan still had available. It could have been that way with sin's ultimate weapon of death. No matter how much good Jesus had done, it would all be lost now if he had been imprisoned by death.

But he hadn't. As the hymnwriter put it:

> 'Death cannot keep his prey,
> Jesus, my Saviour;
> He tore the bars away,
> Jesus my Lord.
>
> Up from the grave he arose...'

Man has hope. Sin's greatest weapon of death was not enough to hold Jesus. The resurrection is proof that sin's power is broken.

3) It is proof that heaven's door is open. Sometimes one child at school will be allowed to play with the 'big boys'. Is that because he's special, important, or looks more grown-up than his class-mates? No, all it means is he's got an older brother and because he's with him he's able to do things from which he'd otherwise be barred.

It's rather like that when Paul describes how those with Christ can now be sure of access to heaven. "Christ has indeed been raised from the dead, the firstfruits of those who have fallen asleep... But each in his own turn: Christ, the firstfruits; then, when he comes, those who belong to him" (verses 20,23). Jesus has been raised and gone on to heaven; all who are identified with him will follow later. He's like the leader in a group cutting a path through near-impenetrable jungle. It's hard work up front hacking the undergrowth away. But once the leader has done that, everyone who takes his path finds the way already cleared for him. Jesus' resurrection was the first journey down the path to glory. Now there's no obstacle to following for those "in Christ" (verse 22). Jesus has blazed the trail to heaven.

Read also: 1 Corinthians 15:3-8

31
NEW LIFE NOW AND ALWAYS
(Colossians 3:1-4)

¹Since, then, you have been raised with Christ, set your hearts on things above, where Christ is seated at the right hand of God. ²Set your minds on things above, not on earthly things. ³For you died, and your life is now hidden with Christ in God. ⁴When Christ, who is your life, appears, then you also will appear with him in glory.

Paul spells out here some reasons why a Christian cannot live as he did before he came to faith in Jesus.

1) New goals. In pre-Christian days these people made decisions based on ordinary needs and wants: food, drink, friendship, love. Sometimes their impulses led to wrong results like greed or immorality. (Paul lists a catalogue of sins from verse 5 onwards.) Problems arose because their lives were based on "earthly things" (verse 2), with no thought to what mattered for eternal life.

Now, as Christians, they're functioning on a new level. Therefore they must switch their thinking, and set their minds "on things above" (verse 1). If someone is promoted at work, he has new responsibilities and does new tasks. Christ has promoted these people to a new life. New values, goals, and behaviour are needed.

2) New environment. Promotion in a career probably brings a new place of work: new building, new office, new colleagues. Being "raised with Christ" equally brings a new environment for life. Paul says, "...you died, and your life is now hidden with Christ in God" (verse 3).

To be "hidden...in God" is a strange phrase. It might be borrowed from Greek culture. When someone died and was buried, the Greeks said he was 'hidden in the earth'. His body was covered and concealed by the ground. Whether Paul has adapted their phrase or not, he certainly has a parallel sense of Christians being dead in respect of their old lives, and now being covered, being enclosed by God. His letters are filled with phrases like "in Christ" or "in God", expressing an almost mystical union with the Lord.

A new environment also means change. If people who are used to living in our atmosphere (with its oxygen, carbon dioxide, and other elements) shifted to another planet with a different atmosphere, they'd have to adapt quickly or die. Christians, now hidden in God, likewise must change. Their way of life - thoughts, words, and deeds - must harmonise with the Lord to whom they are joined.

3) New destiny. A passenger on a bus journey may suddenly realise he wants to travel further. So he asks the conductor or driver for a new ticket. After that he's still on the same bus but he has a new destination. And the Christian remains in the same world, but now - with a 'ticket' paid for him by Jesus - he's heading for a new destination. Paul describes that in verse 4 as sharing the glory of Christ.

Having that destiny ahead changes life now. One of Queen Elizabeth II's three sons always had a different upbringing from his brothers. Charles knew from his youngest days that one day he would be king, and that affected everything he did. Similarly, heaven remains ahead for Christians, but those who mean to share the glory of Christ will already be living as sons of God. Their lives now reflect the destiny which is theirs.

Read also: Romans 6:5-14

32
COURAGE TO WITNESS
(Mark 1:14-15)

14After John was put in prison, Jesus went into Galilee, proclaiming the good news of God. 15"The time has come," he said. "The kingdom of God is near. Repent and believe the good news!"

Usually the first words of verse 14 aren't noticed. Mentally we leap from Jesus' baptism and temptations in the wilderness straight to his early ministry, including the call of the first disciples. Mark, however, noted carefully that Jesus began his public ministry just as John was arrested.

What courage that must have taken for Jesus. He would be well aware that John's arrest was because his preaching had ruffled feathers. His most powerful enemy was King Herod, alienated because John had condemned his marriage to his brother's wife. Herod silenced John by throwing him into a dungeon, from which there was never any likelihood of coming out alive. (Chapter 6:14-29 tells the story of John's death.)

None of that was lost on Jesus. John was paying the price of honest preaching. And yet, even as he heard the news of John's arrest, Jesus began to preach. He would not and could not hold back. This was now the time for him to begin the ministry given to him by God, and he must fulfil it whatever the cost.

What's more his preaching had as much bite as John's. The same cutting edge of warnings of judgment mixed with a call to faith was there. "The kingdom of God is near.

Repent and believe the good news!" (verse 15 - so like John's preaching summed up in verse 4). There was no compromising of the message, no surrender to fear or popular opinion.

The same boldness characterised the early Christians. When Paul lay in chains in a Roman jail for declaring the gospel, he wrote to the church at Ephesus. He asked them to pray for him. He didn't ask for a politician's skill to manipulate words and thus wriggle out of trouble. Nor did he ask them to pray his captors would go easy on him. What he said was: "Pray also for me, that whenever I open my mouth, words may be given me so that I will fearlessly make known the mystery of the gospel, for which I am an ambassador in chains. Pray that I may declare it fearlessly, as I should" (Ephesians 6:19-20).

There are lands today where Christians still risk going to jail for speaking of Jesus. Even in countries where arrest is unlikely there are powerful pressures to keep quiet. Public opinion remains unsympathetic to those who would share their faith. Some people are offended, thinking that no-one has a right to tell others how they should live or what they should believe; some laugh at those who witness, as if faith is infantile and naive in a scientific age; a few become outrightly hostile, responding with verbal, social, and even physical abuse.

Speaking God's truth, then, is never easy. Jesus began preaching when John was arrested. He set his face to do God's work whatever it meant. Ultimately it meant the cross. God's people today have no rights to walk an easier road than that of their Lord. There can be no comfortable Christianity. Courage is still an essential ingredient of discipleship.

Read also: Acts 4:23-31

33
YOUR LIFE IN HIS HANDS
(Jeremiah 29:11)

"For I know the plans I have for you," declares the Lord,
"plans to prosper you and not to harm you, plans to give you
hope and a future."

If ever a verse of the Bible ought to bring us encouragement
it's this one.

1) God has plans for us. There is nothing haphazard
about our lives. Events that seem random in fact have a
purpose.

Tip the pieces of a jigsaw puzzle out of their box into one
large heap on a table, and all you see is an apparently
random mixture of different shapes and colours. Superficially there's no link between them. Yet the truth which
spurs on the jigsaw fanatic is that these pieces do link
together. How they join is not obvious, but he knows the
manufacturer made them to a plan - he even has a picture
of it - and if he keeps going carefully, slowly he'll find the
connections.

God promises us here that he knows what he's doing
with our lives. Even though events seem puzzling and
strange, God has a plan. Safe in that knowledge, we can go
forward, trusting him.

2) God's plans are to bless us. God is good and therefore all he does is good. He can never do anything bad.
That truth is reflected here in the promise that God's plans
will not harm us. Rather he means to prosper our lives,
giving us hope and a future. Whatever God's plans, they're

worth living for. No-one should take that simplistically as a guarantee of health and wealth. God's gift of prosperity cannot be reduced to man's materialistic definitions. His Son lived constantly under his Father's blessing, but had no home or money of his own. He always did God's will yet it allowed persecution, suffering and death. Yet, all the Father wanted was accomplished through the Son. Even the seeming tragedy of his death brought salvation to men and was followed by resurrection for Jesus. The right road was a hard road, but its destination was always glory.

Some today face desperately difficult situations: serious illness; marriage problems; unemployment; family separation; financial crises; tough decisions. God's word to such people is clear. He has a plan for their lives, and it is not a plan to harm them. Rather he wants to give them hope through the knowledge that there is a good future ahead.

3) God's plans to bless us are known to him. This final point must be made. Sometimes our experiences of hardship and suffering make us feel life is either meaningless or that some kind of fate is against us. That's because we can't see any way forward. We cannot envisage anything good coming out of present circumstances, and we find it hard to believe what we cannot see.

Two words in this verse are vital, though. "*I know*," says God. "*I know* the plans I have for you..."

Some large parks or stately homes have a maze made of tall hedges with narrow paths between them. The fun for visitors is to find their way through the maze to the centre. Then what can be just as hard is getting out! Some wander round and round, each path looking the same. They could do that for hours. When someone is completely lost, though, he can shout for help. A guide will then stand on a raised platform with a view over the whole maze and call directions. The lost visitor still has no idea where he is, but the guide does. If the visitor will listen to the directions called to him, then the guide who has the complete picture of the maze will get him soon to safety.

We have a God of love and power. He is Lord of the universe and Lord of our lives. He has the whole picture, and the ability to put us in the right place at the right time to fulfil his will. Therefore, he deserves our trust. We may still not see where we are going. But surely, steadily, he will be guiding us and his firm promise is that his plans will give us hope and a future.

Read also: Philippians 1:12-26

34
SPIRITUAL GROWTH
(Psalm 86:10-13)

¹⁰For you are great and do marvellous deeds;
   you alone are God.
¹¹Teach me your way, O Lord,
   and I will walk in your truth;
give me an undivided heart,
   that I may fear your name.
¹²I will praise you, O Lord my God, with all my heart;
   I will glorify your name for ever.
¹³For great is your love towards me;
   you have delivered me from the depths of the grave.

This is a prayer, but only verse 11 asks for anything. The Psalmist, clearly devoted to his Lord, wants to grow to greater maturity in his walk with God. See what he prays.

1) Teach me. This is about the simplest and most direct request there can be. A father has shown his little boy for the first time how to blow bubbles. The child's arms stretch up, and he cries out, "Daddy, teach me! Teach me!"

And here is someone crying out to God with the same directness and simplicity. His faith isn't only in his head, nor does he treat it as merely a serious hobby. He wants to please his heavenly Father by growing to be a better disciple. "Teach me," he prays.

2) Teach me your way, O Lord. Two words carry special emphasis here. This man of prayer wants to know 'your' way - God's way. His focus isn't on the opinions of others nor on anything to which he might be attracted with his own desires. That's because he recognises God as 'Lord', and therefore God alone has the right to direct his life.

That phrase with its two key words - *your* way, O *Lord* describes the essential attitude of anyone who would grow in his faith. Therefore there'll be little growth for the person who thinks he already knows it all, or reckons his own ideas best, or will follow the crowd. And real discipleship is not only wanting God as Saviour to rescue us from our sins; it must also include accepting God as Lord to direct our lives his way.

3) Teach me your way, O Lord, and I will walk in your truth. Knowledge is one thing; applying that knowledge is quite another. If anyone doubts that let him ponder it next time he accelerates past an amber or red traffic light, nips out in front of traffic at a road junction, or adds a few miles per hour on to the permitted speed limit. He knows what's right - at one time sufficiently well to satisfy an examiner - but driving like that from day to day is another matter. In truth, we all fail to apply the knowledge we have in countless areas of life.

But here is a man praying to God to know his way, and also promising to do it. Head knowledge will not suffice; he must walk in that truth. To love his Lord and Master is to practise what he is taught by him. James writes: "Do not merely listen to the word... Do what it says" (James 1:22). Hundreds of years earlier, the Psalmist also understood that principle.

No relationship matures without effort. With his desire to be taught, to be taught God's way, and with the determination to put that teaching into action, this man's prayer points the way to growth.

Read also: Hebrews 5:11-6:3

35
GODLINESS
(1 Timothy 4:7-10)

⁷Have nothing to do with godless myths and old wives' tales; rather, train yourself to be godly. ⁸For physical training is of some value, but godliness has value for all things, holding promise for both the present life and the life to come.

⁹This is a trustworthy saying that deserves full acceptance ¹⁰(and for this we labour and strive), that we have put our hope in the living God, who is the Saviour of all men, and especially of those who believe.

Most people are capable of doing many different things with their lives. Therefore, making the right choice must be of highest importance. For example, in his college days Jack Nicklaus was no mean basketball player. Neither, of course, was he bad as a golfer. He couldn't make a career out of both, so he had to choose. If he'd chosen basketball, at best he'd have been one among thousands of very average players. Instead he became a professional golfer, winning twenty major tournaments and (in most people's opinion) being ranked as the greatest player ever.

Paul's concern for Timothy was that he should make the right choice. He portrays the alternatives here in broad terms. On one side there are godless myths and old wives' tales. On the other is godliness. In fact, Paul doesn't contrast godliness only with evil and foolish things but with positive and valuable activities like physical training. Whatever the comparison, his point is that godliness comes out on top because it benefits both this life and the next.

The word 'godliness' literally means respect or reverence. In a religious context the respect and reverence are toward God. That's why godliness has eternal as well as temporal value. Nothing else can deliver the double package of benefit for this life and the next.

But are there also other reasons why Paul was so concerned that Timothy should choose godliness? Why must it come at the top of the list?

1) Because it is God's due. Godliness is the only proper manner of behaviour before him.

When the Queen visits a town, no expense is spared and no effort is too great to make everything fit for her visit. Flags are strung across the street, the red carpet rolled out, the brass band plays, and civic officials appear in new and costly suits. The ladies curtsy and men bow. Gracious speeches are made, and children give gifts. And all this is right. The Queen is the sovereign of the land. It would be wrong not to recognise and honour her. The loving and respectful actions of the townspeople and their officials are appropriate. This is her due.

If that is the right behaviour of subjects toward their sovereign, how much greater ought to be the respect and reverence of subjects for the Sovereign of the whole universe? In the presence of God there is a right way to behave.

If God did not exist mankind might as well indulge in myths, tales, and even self-worship. But because there is a God who made and sustains the earth and each person in it, lives ought to be characterised by godliness. Paul knew that, and urged Timothy both to recognise and practise it.

2) Because it is right for man. One of the early lessons learned by a recruit to the army is that each man has his own rank. It's not long before he knows what the different stripes mean on the uniform, whom he must salute, and from whom he takes orders. There is a strict authority system in the army, rigorously enforced. It's not hard to see why. In the midst of battle each man must know and follow his orders. Is he to advance, hold ground, or retreat? If everyone's opinion was as good as any other, then there would be no decisive action. The enemy would sweep forward, and defeat and death would be inevitable. Each man must know his place if there is to be success.

Much that is wrong with this world happens because that principle is rejected for ordinary life. Each thinks he knows best and even calls what he wants his right. If that clashes with what another wants then let the strongest win. The result is a world of greed, hate, dishonesty, and violence. What other outcome could there be when every man shows respect and reverence only for himself?

Old fashioned watches broke down if the cogs and wheels failed to intermesh. Each part had to be linked to the next. That interlinking of one person to another is what's missing from the world when everyone goes his own way. The result is a broken down world. God made us and knows how we are meant to work. True respect for God puts each man back in his rightful and unique place. When his life relates properly to God it also intermeshes with his fellow man. There is no peace or real success any other way.

When man reverences his Maker - practices godliness - then he not only gives God his due but begins to experience that life to the full which Jesus promised to each who would follow him (John 10:10). No wonder Paul urged this young man to choose godliness.

Read also: 1 Timothy 6:3-12

36
COME, FOLLOW ME
(Mark 1:16-18)

16As Jesus walked beside the Sea of Galilee, he saw Simon and his brother Andrew casting a net into the lake, for they were fishermen. 17"Come, follow me," Jesus said, "and I will make you fishers of men." 18At once they left their nets and followed him.

These three verses early in Mark's gospel take us to the heart of what it is to be a Christian.

1) Command. "Come, follow me," said Jesus. This was no invitation to adopt a new philosophy on life or take up a fresh political stance. Jesus wasn't asking them to engage in intellectual chess nor to move them to a more radical or conservative world view. Rather, he was speaking with authority, commanding these men to leave their present lifestyle and walk off to a new future with him.

Some have forgotten that's the basis of Christianity. They think of Christianity as one system of ideas among many - a very good system, but nevertheless a system. If asked, "What is a Christian?" they'd answer, "Someone who believes this, this, and this..." Others would reply in terms of a code of behaviour. A Christian is a good person who lives a fine, upstanding, moral life.

Of course a Christian does have beliefs, and of course his way of life matters, but the bottom line of what makes him different from others is that he has obeyed the command of Jesus to follow him.

2) Change. "I will make you..." Jesus went on to say. These men were being commanded to live new lives. That must have seemed frightening. What would it involve? They couldn't know. Besides, they were skilled only at fishing. How could they do anything else?

Someone who drove his car to the shore and kept going, determined he would have his foreign holiday without the expense of airline or liner tickets, might experience a tragic result. Ambition and determination alone cannot make a car float. Only a major conversion can do that.

Equally that's what these disciples needed. So the promise of change immediately follows the command to become a disciple. Elsewhere Jesus called it being "born again" (John 3:3). In other words, the disciple of Jesus enters a whole new life. He becomes a child born of God (John 1:12-13).

Jesus' words also highlight the fact that he decides on the changes. When a jug is being made, who's in charge? Who decides the shape? Is it the clay? Of course not. The potter as creator has the right to decide the outcome of the vessel he's making.

How can there ever be, then, Christians who think they can tell Jesus what changes are acceptable in their lives, and which areas they'd prefer left alone? Who do they think they are? Who do they think they're dealing with? An old hymn points out: "Thou art the potter, I am the clay," and they'd do well to remember that.

Jesus says, "I will make you..." Those words are foundational. Becoming a disciple means change, and Jesus shapes that change.

3) Purpose. Jesus changes people in order to make them "fishers of men". Probably every Christian would agree that the good news of salvation should be spread to others. Every gospel commands it: Matthew 28:19 "Go and make disciples"; Mark 16:15 "Go into all the world and preach the good news to all creation"; Luke 24:47 "...repentance and forgiveness of sins will be preached in his name to all nations"; John 15:27 "You also must testify...". It would be a rash Christian who would deny the priority of sharing the faith with others. Yet, strangely, few seem to be evangelised. Why?

Every day an old angler called Harry took up his spot by the riverbank and lay out his tackle. His rod and reel were expensive but the best, chosen after searching countless shops and fishermen's magazines. Then Harry unpacked his landing net, checking that all the stringing was in good condition. He prepared his bait, set up his stool, and sat down for his day by the river. Occasionally other fishermen passed by and old Harry was always ready with a word of encouragement or wisdom. He'd read every manual, and carried the biggest and best of them all in his bag. He studied a new portion every day and didn't mind showing it to others to help them with their fishing.

Come sun-down Harry packed up his tackle and trudged his weary way home. He enjoyed being there every day, but somewhere in his heart was an empty space of disappointment because, for all his knowledge, he never caught any fish. His mates down by the river knew why, and chuckled about it sometimes over a jar in the local hostelry. "Poor old Harry," they'd say. "He knows it all and he's dead keen. But you don't catch fish if you won't cast your line in the water."

"What?" some newcomer would interrupt incredulously. "Harry just leaves his rod lying on the bank each day? Does he expect the fish to jump out of the river straight into his bag?"

With a shake of the head, someone would answer, "Harry's simply too frightened he might damage his perfect rod, his line, or his net. He worries in case the hook tangles in the weed, the rod snaps, or perhaps the string on the net tears. They're all silly fears, of course, but Harry prefers just to go home and tell his wife it's been another unlucky day."

Poor Harry... But perhaps he's not so very different from many Christians who know the need to take risks to witness to family, neighbours, or colleagues, but won't do it. Could it be that one of the best kept secrets of Christianity is that the majority of Christians know only the theory of sharing their faith?

4) Response. "At once they left their nets and followed him" (verse 18). Jesus issued a command, promised a change, gave a purpose, and it was met with a response. Three things are obvious about it.

a) It was immediate. These men went with Jesus straight away. There was no hesitation. They couldn't have realised yet that he was God's Son, but still sensed his divine authority and reacted instantly.

b) It was costly. When they left their nets they left their income. Their only security in life lay in their fishing business. But nothing was more important than the call of Jesus (Luke 14:33).

c) It was final. There was no going back. Once they walked away from the Sea of Galilee to catch men instead of fish their lives could never be the same again. There could be no trial period to see if they liked it. It was all or nothing.

These men could have stayed in the water and gone on catching fish, ignoring the extravagant demands of this stranger on the shore. If Simon and Andrew had done that, probably they'd have enjoyed their work, brought up families, and made enough money to keep them all comfortable. But by coming ashore and going with Jesus they found an eternal life more valuable than anything fishing could ever have given. What's more, in catching men they began to change the world. What they lost was nothing compared with those gains.

It began - as it does still - with obeying the call of Jesus.

Read also: Acts 9:1-19

37
GREAT IS THY FAITHFULNESS
(Lamentations 3:22-26)

^{22}Because of the Lord's great love we are not consumed,
*   for his compassions never fail.*
^{23}They are new every morning;
*   great is your faithfulness.*
^{24}I say to myself, "The Lord is my portion;
*   therefore I will wait for him."*
^{25}The Lord is good to those whose hope is in him,
*   to the one who seeks him;*
^{26}it is good to wait quietly
*   for the salvation of the Lord.*

Some will not have realised that the roots of the hymn *Great is Thy faithfulness* lie in the Book of Lamentations. But here they are, full of positive encouragement.

1) They teach that God can be relied on. It's because of God's love and faithfulness, both described as "great", that man survives. Man's failures would destroy him, but God won't let that happen. It's like a child learning to swim, all the time with his father's hand poised just underneath in case he sinks. The father cares for his son, and won't let him drown.

Every day God is like that. He doesn't give up on us even when we keep making mistakes. His "compassions never fail" and are "new every morning". What security we have with a God of such "great faithfulness" as this.

2) They teach that God should be sought. To "wait for" the Lord sounds like a good excuse to do nothing. Here we're not only told that, but even to "wait quietly" for his salvation. Some Christians today are so passive and quiet about their faith that it would be a real surprise to meet them in heaven.

In fact the writer qualifies his meaning with the statement, "The Lord is good to those whose hope is in him, to the one who seeks him..." God's compassions aren't dropped on an inactive, idle soul, but are given to the one looking to him. Picture a nestful of baby birds "waiting" to be fed. They're not snoozing. Mouths are gaping, and as mother bird returns with food they clamour desperately for their beaks to be filled. The promise, then, is that those who seek God like that will never be disappointed. His great faithfulness is for them.

Read also: Psalm 34:1-10

38
WORSHIPPING GOD
(Psalm 47)

¹Clap your hands, all you nations;
  shout to God with cries of joy.
²How awesome is the Lord Most High,
  the great King over all the earth!
³He subdued nations under us,
  peoples under our feet.
⁴He chose our inheritance for us,
  the pride of Jacob, whom he loved.
                              Selah

⁵God has ascended amid shouts of joy,
  the Lord amid the sounding of trumpets.
⁶Sing praises to God, sing praises;
  sing praises to our King, sing praises.

⁷For God is the King of all the earth;
  sing to him a psalm of praise.
⁸God reigns over the nations;
  God is seated on his holy throne.
⁹The nobles of the nations assemble
  as the people of the God of Abraham,
for the kings of the earth belong to God;
  he is greatly exalted.

For many Christians worship is a rather drab and uninspiring business. When the minister says, "Let us worship God," the heads go down and usually the hearts with them. The worship shown in this Psalm is very different from that.

1) Worship is excited and noisy. The hymn writer (using biblical words) wrote: 'Worship the Lord in the beauty of holiness.' Some quote that to describe the architecture of a church sanctuary; others use it to justify quiet, meditative, hymn or Psalm singing. In fact, the beauty of holiness has nothing to do with building design or musical volume. It has everything to do with attitude of heart.

Psalm 47 shows worshippers whose hearts are bursting with excitement. There's an explosion of praise to God as the people clap their hands and shout their joy to God (verse 1). Accompanied by more shouting, the trumpets blast (verse 5), and the people are swept along in wave after wave of praise (verse 6). Their awareness of God's magnificence evokes all this excitement and noise.

If a crowd can sing, cheer, and shout for 22 men kicking a piece of leather on a football pitch, surely God's people can better than match their enthusiasm since their God is so much more worthy of adoration. The Book of Revelation portrays heaven as filled with noisy praise. 'In a loud voice they sang...' writes John (Revelation 5:12). Those who know God already should be experiencing something of that excited joy in his presence even now.

2) Worship exalts God alone. Sometimes a child will leave a friend's birthday party moaning, "That wasn't much fun. They never played the games I like." But so what? Surely what matters is that the birthday child had the games *he* wanted, and that *he* enjoyed himself. The moaners have the wrong centre of attention. That's often the problem of those who say after church, "I didn't get much from that." The real question is, "Did *God* get much from us - our love, adoration, praise, and submission?"

In this Psalm there's almost nothing about the feelings

of the worshippers other than their sense of awe at being in the presence of such a great God (verse 2). He is the centre of attention in every sentence in the Psalm. Every heart was turned to him. Everyone was concerned to give to him a gift of praise worthy of the Lord Most High.

A wedding photograph is unacceptable if the bride and groom are out of focus. Aunt Agatha may be pinsharp, but (despite what she thinks) she's not the one who matters on that day. The wedding couple must be seen clearly. Equally no-one can worship God meaningfully until he learns how to focus on the subject which matters.

3) Worship expresses his greatness and goodness. These people were acutely conscious of who their God was and what he had done. They saw him as 'the great King over all the earth' (verse 2). They knew 'God reigns over the nations; God is seated on his holy throne' (verse 8). Every world leader, noble or king, belongs to God. He is exalted over all of them (verse 9). His goodness was clear in the way he had led Israel in the past. God had brought them from captivity and settled them in a new land. That was his gift to people he loved (verses 3 and 4).

Consciousness of that kind of greatness and goodness in God ignited their worship as surely as a spark ignites dry grass. Once the fire of praise had begun, and as they experienced more of this God, the worship could only burn brighter and stronger.

Such real worship - excited, exalting - came from people who didn't know God's clearer revelation of himself through Jesus. We do, so our worship should even exceed theirs. Heaven will be filled with perfect praise, and what we bring now in worship might be only a dim reflection of that, but at least it should be a reflection.

Read also: Revelation 5:11-14

39
YOUR MONEY AND YOUR LIFE
(Mark 10:17-22)

[17]As Jesus started on his way, a man ran up to him and fell on his knees before him. "Good teacher," he asked, "what must I do to inherit eternal life?"

[18]"Why do you call me good?" Jesus answered. "No-one is good - except God alone. [19]You know the commandments: 'Do not murder, do not commit adultery, do not steal, do not give false testimony, do not defraud, honour your father and mother.'"

[20]"Teacher," he declared, "all these I have kept since I was a boy." [21]Jesus looked at him and loved him. "One thing you lack," he said. "Go, sell everything you have and give to the poor, and you will have treasure in heaven. Then come, follow me."

[22]At this the man's face fell. He went away sad, because he had great wealth.

Shops have sales because there are times of the year, especially in early January and mid-summer, when people won't pay the normal price for goods. In order to sell their stock, the shops must drop the price to a level people are willing to pay. In respect of discipleship, that's precisely what Jesus would not do.

This young man came to him with enthusiasm (ran up to him), with dedication (fell on his knees before him), respect (Good teacher), and sincerely wanted to discover spiritual truth (what must I do to inherit eternal life?). From the conversation which followed it's obvious that he had a high commitment to God already. He could say with honesty that he'd kept the commandments since boyhood.

However, Jesus saw one great weakness in him. The man was in love with his wealth. It was a god to him. But the very first commandment said: 'You shall have no other gods before me' (Exodus 20:3). Therefore, Jesus told him, to have eternal life he should give his money away to the poor and then follow him. That way he'd have treasure in heaven. And the young man wouldn't do it. His money was so important to him he couldn't part with it.

Jesus certainly didn't want to part with him either. He was interested, sincere, and probably well educated and talented. Something about his honest seeking touched Jesus' heart ('Jesus looked at him and loved him'). Many another preacher would have run after such a young man. Maybe he'd have told the youth he only had to be willing to sell everything, not actually do it. But Jesus let him go. He couldn't lower the terms of commitment for anyone. The cost was always, 'any of you who does not give up everything he has cannot be my disciple' (Luke 14:33). No sale terms were available. The full price had to be paid by this man too, or there could be no eternal life.

Fireworks zoom into the night sky, mushroom into a cloud of glorious colour and then disappear into the darkness. Much the same happens with some who appear so keen on the Christian faith initially but give up after a time. Perhaps their sudden demise is because they've finally found out the cost of commitment, and they're not willing for Jesus to be Lord of every part of their lives. They have loves greater than their love for him. They should have known from the beginning, but sooner or later everyone discovers that real discipleship is possible only at full cost.

Read also: Luke 14:25-27

40
PLANNING THE FUTURE
(James 4:13-17)

13Now listen, you who say, "Today or tomorrow we will go to this or that city, spend a year there, carry on business and make money." 14Why, you do not even know what will happen tomorrow. What is your life? You are a mist that appears for a little while and then vanishes. 15Instead, you ought to say, "If it is the Lord's will, we will live and do this or that." 16As it is, you boast and brag. All such boasting is evil. 17Anyone, then, who knows the good he ought to do and doesn't do it, sins.

Wise businessmen plan for the future, but they do it cautiously because they know there is much over which they have little control: supplies of materials, inflation and the general economic climate, interest rates, industrial unrest, and so on. A manager could set a course and then find his business in trouble if raw materials become scarce or more expensive. He can't 'manage' all the factors, therefore he goes forward carefully.

James teaches a similar point for ordinary living. When we make plans there ought to be wise caution. We must never forget that we cannot give ourselves (or others) guarantees about the future.

We often fail to remember that. Our arrogance breeds an over-confidence which thinks that to have planned something is as good as to have done it. We speak as if intentions equalled accomplishments (verse 13). In fact, that is no more than boasting - evil, unwise, presumptuous boasting (verse 16). What we've failed to recognise is our ignorance, for we don't know the content of even the next twenty four hours never mind the next year or longer (verse 14). Who can be sure that an accident or illness won't come, or that some new priority won't arise?

In place of arrogance and in recognition of inevitable ignorance, James suggests two alternative attitudes.

1) **Humility.** We should see that our lives have no more permanence and stability than a mist, something easily blown away (verse 14). Like it or not, there are things which even the most intellectual or powerful of men cannot oppose. For example, many a millionaire, with unlimited finance and very influential friends, has lain dying finally acknowledging that ill-health or old age were forces he could not control. A wiser man would have recognised his limited powers much earlier, and lived his life in humility.

2) **Submission.** James points out that the Lord's will - not ours - will always come out on top (verse 15). 'Man proposes, but God disposes,' is an old saying. So is Proverbs 16:9, "In his heart a man plans his course, but the Lord determines his steps." No matter what someone plans, God has the last word.

That should not encourage fatalism, the belief that 'fate' controls what happens in life. Rather, control rests in the hands of a mighty and loving God, someone who can be trusted for the direction he takes us in life.

A father tells his son, "We're going out together tomorrow."

"Where to?" asks the boy.

"I can't tell you yet," replies Dad, "but I promise it'll be good."

And that's enough for the son. Tomorrow he'll go off

with his father, brimming with eagerness and excitement, knowing his father loves him and that he'll have a wonderful time. He hasn't been told where he's going or what he'll do, but Dad knows, and Dad can be trusted.

James teaches a similar submission to God. He knows what's best and what's right. Yes, we may plan, but those plans must be laid before the Father, trusting that whatever he allows will be good.

Read also: Luke 12:16-21

41
LEADER: PUBLIC ENEMY NO.1
(Exodus 5:1-21)

¹Afterwards Moses and Aaron went to Pharaoh and said, "This is what the Lord, the God of Israel, says: 'Let my people go, so that they may hold a festival to me in the desert.'"

²Pharaoh said, "Who is the Lord, that I should obey him and let Israel go? I do not know the Lord and I will not let Israel go."

³Then they said, "The God of the Hebrews has met with us. Now let us take a three-day journey into the desert to offer sacrifices to the Lord our God, or he may strike us with plagues or with the sword."

⁴But the king of Egypt said, "Moses and Aaron, why are you taking the people away from their labour? Get back to your work!" ⁵Then Pharaoh said, "Look, the people of the land are now numerous, and you are stopping them from working."

⁶That same day Pharaoh gave this order to the slave drivers and foremen in charge of the people: ⁷"You are no longer to supply the people with straw for making bricks; let them go and gather their own straw ⁸But require them to make the same number of bricks as before; don't reduce the quota. They are lazy; that is why they are crying out, 'Let us go and sacrifice to our God.' ⁹Make the work harder for the men so that they keep working and pay no attention to lies."

¹⁰Then the slave drivers and the foremen went out and said to the people, "This is what Pharaoh says: 'I will not give you any more straw. ¹¹Go and get your own straw wherever you can find it, but your work will not be reduced at all.'" [12]So the people scattered all over Egypt to gather stubble to use for straw. [13]The slave drivers kept pressing them, saying, "Complete the work required of you for each day, just as when you had straw." [14]The Israelite foremen appointed by Pharaoh's slave drivers were beaten and were asked, "Why didn't you meet your quota of bricks yesterday or today, as before?"

[15]Then the Israelite foremen went and appealed to Pharaoh: "Why have you treated your servants this way? [16]Your servants are given no straw, yet we are told, 'Make bricks!' Your servants are being beaten, but the fault is with your own people."

[17]Pharaoh said, "Lazy, that's what you are - lazy! That is why you keep saying, 'Let us go and sacrifice to the Lord.' [18]Now get to work. You will not be given any straw, yet you must produce your full quota of bricks."

[19]The Israelite foremen realised they were in trouble when they were told, "You are not to reduce the number of bricks required of you for each day." [20]When they left Pharaoh, they found Moses and Aaron waiting to meet them, [21]and they said, "May the Lord look upon you and judge you! You have made us a stench to Pharaoh and his officials and have put a sword in their hand to kill us."

Moses had not been back in Egypt for long. It was an unwilling return and he'd argued against it. But God doesn't negotiate. Moses had to go. However, at least he'd come with an overwhelming commission from God. All this must have encouraged him, and his hopes for success are high as he goes to see Pharaoh.

That optimism is soon smashed when the *first reaction* of the Egyptian king is refusal. Moses and Aaron declare God's command to let the people go (verse 1) but he states boldly that he doesn't know the Lord and will not set them free (verse 2). Moreover, Moses and Aaron are warned about putting the people off their work (verses 4-5). So far the two liberators have achieved nothing except to receive a rebuke.

Quite often Christians testify that they knew they were in the will of God in some matter because 'everything fell into place'. This and that worked out perfectly, so God had to be in it. Well, if circumstances and events coming together neatly is the indicator of being in God's will, then many of God's saints including Moses must have been well out of it. Not even Jesus had everything work out straight-forwardly for him. A friend betrayed him and opponents put him to death. The truth is that being in the will of God has little to do with whether the journey through life is smooth or bumpy. God has made no promises to take away hardships, tensions, and difficulties. By contrast, doing God's will may give us these things, although his help is also there to bring us through them. If your life is more like a hurdle race than a flat sprint don't give up. The obstacles don't mean you must be outside God's will.

Pharaoh goes further than denying Moses' request. His *second reaction* is to make life tougher for the Israelites by removing their supply of straw but compelling the same quota of bricks to be made (verses 6-9). Their foremen are beaten when the workers don't produce the quota. Upset, they appeal to Pharaoh for an explanation (verses 15-16). In response they're told that no straw will be given to them because of their laziness. They can't have much work to do if they can think of going off to make sacrifices to God. They can use that time instead to fetch their own straw and still produce the same number of bricks (verses 17-18).

The people are outraged, of course, and round on

Moses and Aaron for making their lives harder. They're told that, far from helping, their actions risk the slaughter of the whole nation (verses 20-21).

How devastating that reaction from the Israelite foremen must have been for Moses. He had risked his life to set foot in Egypt again. He'd come back only because he cared for these people and believed it was God's will to set them free. Now it's all gone wrong. They've turned on him, and instead of saving them he may have caused them to be wiped out.

The person who would be a leader of God's people cannot be a fragile ornament, easily smashed by the first tremors of trouble. These accusations against Moses were unfair and cruel but still they were made. Everything he'd done was God's will but it didn't win support even from those for whom he risked his life. Moses had 'rocked the boat', and initially that made life tougher for the Israelites. No matter how good his intentions, they didn't like that. And they didn't hesitate to tell him.

A wise leader doesn't ignore hostile statements. That would be arrogance. (Moses immediately went to God in prayer when he was accused - verses 22 and 23.) But neither does he naively accept every criticism and give up. God's call remains. Fulfilling it may mean the leader has to sacrifice popularity, his inner desire to be loved by everyone. That's hard, but it's part of the price of leadership.

Read also: 2 Timothy 2:1-7

42
ANTIDOTE TO FEAR
(Psalm 46:10)

Be still, and know that I am God;
  I will be exalted among the nations,
  I will be exalted in the earth.

The people of Israel were going through tough times. They were facing wars and other disasters. The temptation to doubt and panic was strong - everything seemed out of their control. It was. But, thankfully, none of it was out of God's control. He speaks directly to them in this Psalm, and in less than ten words gives them the antidote to all their fear, "Be still, and know that I am God."

1) Be still. Rushing around, brain racing from one possible solution to the next, getting one opinion after another hoping one must be right... Faced with problems, that's what we do. We're like a trapped fly throwing itself constantly against a window in its desperation to escape. If only that fly would settle for a moment. Then it might see an open window and get its freedom.

God would have us calm down. Instead of being deafened by so many voices and exhausted by so many possibilities, he'd have us be still: still to listen for his voice, still to wait for his solution.

How frustrating we find it when someone won't pause long enough in what he's asking to listen to the answer. We'd love to tell him, if only we could get a word in edgeways. God has answers for us. Too often, though, we don't pause to hear him because we're so preoccupied with our own words and actions. "Be still," says God. That's the essential beginning to finding his solution to our problems and fears.

2) Be still and know that I am God. When we stop rushing around, and take a good look with the eyes of faith, we begin to see our fears in their true perspective. We'd thought them mountains when they were only mole-hills. We'd imagined there was no way through when the truth was just that we couldn't see it.

Abraham and Sarah were sure they could never have children. They were so sure that foolishly they arranged for Hagar, Sarah's maid, to be the world's first surrogate mother, and Abraham had Ishmael as a son with her. That brought nothing but heartache. If only, instead of impatiently trying out their own solution, they'd been still and realised who was God and what he could do. When finally they did listen to him, they heard him say, "Is anything too hard for the Lord? I will return to you at the appointed time next year and Sarah will have a son" (Genesis 18:14). And so Abraham aged 100 and Sarah aged 90 finally had their own child. Instead of thinking they had to solve all problems themselves, with their own feeble powers, now they learned who really ruled the universe. They had a new perspective.

Fear thrives on the belief that a situation is out of control. It's hopeless; nothing can be done. That's true only if God is left out. God's word to "Be still, and know that I am God" is a plea to put him foremost in our thinking. That makes all the difference. Nothing is insoluble for him. When we take time to know that he is God, faith is born and fear banished.

Read also: Daniel 3:13-30

43
THE CAPACITY TO CARE
(1 Peter 5:6-7)

6Humble yourselves, therefore, under God's mighty hand, that he may lift you up in due time. 7Cast all your anxiety on him because he cares for you.

If you're in trouble and need assistance, the person you turn to must have two essential characteristics: a) the ability to help, and b) the motivation to help. If the money has run out long before the month has, an equally impoverished friend is little use to you. Neither is someone who is rich if he won't give you a loan. The power and concern to lift you out of trouble are both needed.

Peter encourages his readers by showing that God has both these characteristics. They've been through some exceptionally hard times, especially from persecution (4:12-19). They desperately need help. Now, in these two verses of chapter five, Peter points them to the twin facts that God has a mighty hand and that he cares for them.

That power of God is sufficient to lift up the most bruised and battered of his children. Nothing that has happened to them is beyond his power to heal and restore (verse 10). These Christians must now recognise that and entrust themselves to him. A child walks and walks until his little legs will carry him no more. As he sinks down his father picks him up, holds him close, and carries him home. The father's strength is not exhausted, and he will take him where he has no power to go alone. So these Christians are to humble themselves under God's mighty hand that in due time (not necessarily when they please) he may lift them up.

Thankfully they can have confidence God wants to do that. There is no need for anxiety, because his love motivates him to help. What a remarkable statement Peter makes, that the God of the whole universe should care for each person. When you take time to think about that, it's almost beyond comprehension. Even so, it should never be beyond appreciation. What peace and encouragement it should give to know that this great God wants our happiness and well-being even more than we do. So why fear? If the omnipotent God cares for us, then no situation is hopeless.

Here is a God of might and care, a God of power and love. If we truly know such a God, it's impossible to feel other than safe and secure.

Read also: Matthew 6:25-34

44
LONGING AFTER GOD
(Psalm 84:1-2)

¹How lovely is your dwelling-place,
  O Lord Almighty!
²My soul yearns, even faints,
  for the courts of the Lord;
my heart and my flesh cry out
  for the living God.

This writer looks for any opportunity to be in God's temple courts, but, as verse 2 makes clear, that's only because his real desire is to find God himself. And how deeply he longs for the Lord. His whole life is affected by his need to be with God. His soul yearns and even faints for the place where God's presence is found. His heart and flesh cry out for him. Everything in him wants an encounter with God.

Expressions of desire like this belong in the context of deep relationships. Perhaps a young woman in love thinks constantly of her partner, and feels faint with excitement and anticipation at seeing him again. All day it's hard to concentrate on other things, such is her longing for the time when they'll be together. Everything else pales into insignificance compared to being with her only true love.

The Psalmist feels a similar passion for God. His Lord means that much to him. If we will fill our minds with his greatness, goodness, and love for us, then we'll be gripped with a similar deep stirring of the heart and soul to be with our God.

Read also: Song of Songs 2:3-5

45
WHEN THE GOING GETS TOUGH...
(Acts 6:1-7)

¹In those days when the number of disciples was increasing, the Grecian Jews among them complained against the Hebraic Jews because their widows were being overlooked in the daily distribution of food. ²So the Twelve gathered all the disciples together and said, "It would not be right for us to neglect the ministry of the word of God in order to wait on tables. ³Brothers, choose seven men from among you who are known to be full of the Spirit and wisdom. We will turn this responsibility over to them ⁴and will give our attention to prayer and the ministry of the word."

⁵This proposal pleased the whole group. They chose Stephen, a man full of faith and of the Holy Spirit; also Philip, Procorus, Nicanor, Timon, Parmenas, and Nicolas from Antioch, a convert to Judaism. ⁶They presented these men to the apostles, who prayed and laid their hands on them.

⁷So the word of God spread. The number of disciples in Jerusalem increased rapidly, and a large number of priests became obedient to the faith.

The Bible often records conflict. Those who plead for a return to the 'New Testament church' ought to remember just how problematical that time could be. The first Christians were far from perfect, and those who wrote their story were honest in telling the bad along with the good.

Here the difficulty is an accusation of racial discrimination in the church. All the Christians in these early days were Jews, but some had their homeland in Judea while others were born and raised in other parts of the Mediterranean region. That second group complained of unfair treatment for their widows. Charges of prejudice and injustice flew thick and fast. It was a serious situation, threatening to divide the fledgling church. Notice, then, how the problem was handled.

1) The problem was faced. The first thing the twelve apostles did was bring everyone together to confront what was wrong (verse 2). They could have ignored the dispute, hoping it would just go away. Plenty car owners do that when they hear an ominous rattle from the engine. Instead of heading for a garage, they try not to hear it, and trust that it won't be there next time. Some treat aches, pains, lumps and bumps in their body similarly. Rather than go to a doctor, they simply hope they'll wake up well tomorrow. Many a car owner or sick person has found the delay was fatal.

The same applies in church life. The 'ignore it and hope it'll disappear' mentality is rife. But that changes nothing for the better, and usually leads to even greater problems emerging. Lesson number one from the early church was that when conflict arose the leaders brought the people together in order to deal with it.

2) They chose an appropriate solution. The quickest and easiest way for the apostles to have solved this problem would have been for them to distribute the food themselves. That would have ended the conflict immediately and definitely, for clearly they were held in high regard. What's more, their humility and hard work in taking on such a menial task would have made them look good in everyone's eyes. What an attractive option this must have seemed to the Twelve!

However, to choose that solution would have taken the

apostles away from what only they could do in terms of prayer and teaching. That was their fundamental calling (verses 2, 4). To neglect it might bring short-term gains but certainly also long-term losses for the church.

It may be very nice for an aircraft pilot to keep his passengers informed over the intercom about the scenery below but, if that distracts him to the extent he makes an error in flying the plane and it crashes, then all lose. Only he can fly it; let someone else describe the terrain below. No-one else could lead in prayer and teaching like the apostles. Anyone who was respected by all the community could distribute the food. So the apostles took the risk of delegation, and even had the people choose which seven. That way there could hardly be any argument over their policies. An appropriate solution was found.

3) Only wise, Spirit-filled men were allowed. It's sobering to realise someone needed to be known as full of the Spirit and wisdom (verse 3) just to be a waiter in the early church. We appoint people so casually, and sometimes not for the best of reasons. At one extreme we give positions of church leadership to some as a kind of honour for being a respected person; at the other we scramble to land unwanted tasks on anyone sufficiently foolish or naive to take them.

These first Christians were told to find people of real spiritual maturity even to serve food. They didn't ask, "Has anyone among us ever been a waiter before?" Spiritual qualifications were more important than technical ability for the work. Of course what these men were to do was more than guaranteeing equal portions. They were peacemakers, and they needed sensitivity and godliness. Therefore the priority for the people was to find men who lived close to God. That's a qualification which should be required for any service within God's church.

4) The solution was effective. If someone has an infected wound it's worse than useless to stick a Band-Aid on it. The sticking plaster may hide the sore temporarily, but leaves it to fester away underneath. Often that's our failure with problems in the church. We opt for whatever is least troublesome and least painful. Perhaps we don't want to upset someone who's held a job for forty years. Perhaps we're not prepared to spend money. Perhaps no-one's got time to get involved in restructuring an organisation. Rather than take hard, costly measures we accept short-term answers. Things look better for a time but eventually re-emerge much worse.

That was not so on this occasion in the early church. This conflict was solved. We never read of it again. In fact, verse 7 says the church grew rapidly. A cancer in the Body of Christ had been cured, and therefore the healed Body could be more vigorous than ever. The church today certainly needs new life and growth. Could that goal help us have the courage to apply effective solutions to our problems?

Read also: John 13:34-35

46
THE MEASURE OF HIS LOVE
(John 10:14-18)

¹⁴I am the good shepherd; I know my sheep and my sheep know me - ¹⁵just as the Father knows me and I know the Father - and I lay down my life for the sheep. ¹⁶I have other sheep that are not of this sheep pen. I must bring them also. They too will listen to my voice, and there shall be one flock and one shepherd. ¹⁷The reason my Father loves me is that I lay down my life - only to take it up again. ¹⁸No-one takes it from me, but I lay it down of my own accord. I have authority to lay it down and authority to take it up again. This command I received from my Father.

Who would choose to suffer loss if he had an alternative? For example, who'd want his new car to crash? Or, who'd decide to make a bad investment and have his money diminish in value? Or, who'd opt to become disabled and lose his health? Such things do happen to people, but always unwillingly. No-one means them to happen.

Above all, no-one chooses to die, not if there's any way to avoid it. There are occasional heroic stories of people sacrificing themselves for someone they loved, for someone very important. But these are the exceptions. In general people prefer life; death is an enemy to be avoided.

Jesus was different.

First, he chose to die. He makes it clear in these verses that he didn't need to die. Jesus was never the victim of other people's scheming. He knew the crucifixion was coming, but it was avoidable had he wanted to avoid it.

Rather, Jesus gave his life. "No-one takes it from me, but I lay it down of my own accord" (verse 18). He deliberately accepted death.

In addition, Jesus chose to die for those who hated him. He gave his life for those who disobeyed his teaching, broke his laws, ignored his will, and mocked his name. He died for those who killed him. His death was a deliberate choice to take on himself the sins of ordinary people, people who have failed God in countless ways, small and large. Jesus substituted himself on the cross for them, and took their penalty of death. If the sheep had never strayed, then they would never have been in danger, and the shepherd would not have had to give his own life for them. But they did stray, and Jesus chose to lay down his life for foolish sheep like that (verse 15).

The measure of someone's love is the sacrifice he'll make. At one level, a young lady may decide the extent of a young man's feelings for her according to whether it's an expensive or cheap restaurant to which he takes her! At a far more significant level, here is Jesus choosing the ultimate sacrifice of his own life. He was willing to give that up for people who don't deserve it.

That's the measure of his love for you and me.

Read also: Isaiah 53:3-6

47
FINAL JUDGMENT
(Revelation 20:11-21:4)

[11] Then I saw a great white throne and him who was seated on it. Earth and sky fled from his presence, and there was no place for them. [12] And I saw the dead, great and small, standing before the throne, and books were opened. Another book was opened, which is the book of life. The dead were judged according to what they had done as recorded in the books. [13] The sea gave up the dead that were in it, and death and Hades gave up the dead that were in them, and each person was judged according to what he had done. [14] Then death and Hades were thrown into the lake of fire. The lake of fire is the second death. [15] If anyone's name was not found written in the book of life, he was thrown into the lake of fire.

21 Then I saw a new heaven and a new earth, for the first heaven and the first earth had passed away, and there was no longer any sea. [2] I saw the Holy City, the new Jerusalem, coming down out of heaven from God, prepared as a bride beautifully dressed for her husband. [3] And I heard a loud voice from the throne saying, "Now the dwelling of God is with men, and he will live with them. They will be his people, and God himself will be with them and be their God. [4] He will wipe every tear from their eyes. There will be no more death or mourning or crying or pain, for the old order of things has passed away."

Often we'd like to know at least something about the future. For example, if a final year student could have definite foreknowledge of the job he'd be doing in a year's time he wouldn't need to scour advertisements nor worry about his final exams. If someone could be sure whom he would marry vast amounts of emotional trauma and heartache could be avoided, not to mention expense. The advantage of knowing the future would be the opportunity to alter what we do in the present.

Normally God hides the future from us, but here we're given a glimpse of mankind's future precisely so each person has a chance to change what he believes and does now. God shows us now so that we'll live differently now. What he lets us see are three facts about the end of man.

1) The experience of judgment. This gathering of all people before God is described in other parts of the New Testament too (Matthew 25:31-46; Romans 14:10-12; Hebrews 9:27). God is holy, and therefore will not ignore sin. If there were no accounting, the universe would degenerate into moral anarchy. But there is judgment, and two features of it are especially stressed here.

(a) Judgment is universal. Everyone - "the dead, great and small" - is there before God's throne. The rich and famous stand alongside the poorest of beggars; the most powerful of rulers are alongside the weakest and most despised of men; those who thought themselves good appear along with those whom society has already condemned as wicked. No-one, no matter his money, influence, or popular appeal sidesteps this judgment.

(b) Judgment is fair. "Each person was judged according to what he had done." John sees record books containing details of how each had lived. Some people keep a journal of what they do each day. The imagery used here suggests that everyone is writing a second, secret journal in heaven about their lives. That's what is used as the basis of

judgment. Therefore there are no mistakes. No-one has grounds to complain of unfairness. The judgment received is on the evidence of that person's own record.

2) For some, the experience of judgment is eternal death. One book opened at judgment time is called "the book of life". In the ancient world every city and ruler had a roll-book of living citizens of that city, those who belonged in that kingdom. When a man died his name was removed from the roll.

This book of life is similar. All who are spiritually alive, members of God's kingdom, have their names entered there. Others - the spiritually dead - don't appear in the roll book. Their eternity lies in the "lake of fire", otherwise known as "the second death". They've died once from life on earth; now they die forever. There is no escape. For all eternity they are dead to God, his life, and his goodness. No wonder the Bible elsewhere describes that as great suffering.

No-one likes tragedies; we all want stories with happy endings. There is no happy ending for these people, and the extra dimension of tragedy here is that this never needed to happen. All men have sinned, but none need suffer its consequences. Jesus died on the cross to take their penalty, and the gift of forgiveness is free now for all who will receive it. How sad that so many don't. The drowning man who fights off his rescuer and then perishes had his chance of life, but he threw it away. So with those who experience the second death. They could have lived, but they chose to die.

3) For others, the experience of judgment is eternal life. That's the experience of those whose names are in the book of life. They had not lived up to God's standard any more than those who died eternally, but they'd accepted the outstretched hand of their rescuer. They'd believed in Jesus as Saviour and lived with him as Lord. As disciples of Jesus they were made spiritually alive, and as citizens of God's kingdom had their names put in God's book of the living (Luke 10:20; Philippians 4:3).

What a glorious eternity they have. Chapter 21 describes a new world in which they know God and live in his presence. God himself wipes away their tears, and all that used to hurt them is abolished. The old order has passed; a new order has begun.

No-one can earn this. No-one can pay for it. Thankfully, no-one needs to, for Jesus has already paid the full price for us. He died in our place, taking away our sin, and now gives his goodness to those who believe. In Christ we are accepted by God, made spiritually alive, and can look forward to a final judgment which will bring only life. "For the wages of sin is death, but the gift of God is eternal life in Christ Jesus our Lord" (Romans 6:23).

Read also: Matthew 25:31-46

48
THE POWER OF THE SPIRIT
(Acts 1:4-5,8)

⁴On one occasion, while he was eating with them, he gave them this command: "Do not leave Jerusalem, but wait for the gift my Father promised, which you have heard me speak about. ⁵For John baptised with water, but in a few days you will be baptised with the Holy Spirit...

⁸But you will receive power when the Holy Spirit comes on you; and you will be my witnesses in Jerusalem, and in all Judea and Samaria, and to the ends of the earth."

This must be the only biblical example of a command to Christians not to witness. It's only a temporary halt, of course, not a permanent prohibition. Clearly Jesus wanted these disciples to evangelise, but he most certainly didn't want them trying it in their own strength.

Therefore he tells them to wait for the Holy Spirit. The Spirit is the gift the Father has promised. He's not an afterthought, but always intended by God. It's almost like a boy being told he's to do a demanding job - perhaps digging the back garden - and wondering how he'll ever manage on his own. But then he discovers that his father had always planned to work beside him, and that he would be taking on the really heavy work. What had seemed impossible now becomes realistic. So, for these men, the great commission of Jesus to make disciples of all nations (Matthew 28:19) now makes sense if the same Spirit who was in Jesus will be with them.

In fact, he'll be more than 'with' them. Jesus' promise

is that soon (not yet, interestingly) they'll be baptised with the Holy Spirit. The Greek word we translate 'baptised' was used in Jesus' time to describe ships sinking or people drowning. They were baptised; they went under. The image here, then, is of people being immersed with the Spirit of God.

If a woman decides to dye a coat a new colour, she will fill her bath with the dye and leave the garment in it for hours. Every inch of the coat must be drenched. She wants the new colour to permeate every fibre. That's the kind of meaning which belongs here with the word baptised. That is the depth of the experience of the Spirit Jesus meant for his disciples. Nothing about them was to be unaffected. Their entire beings would be soaked in the Spirit of God, and then they would be able to be his witnesses.

The sharing of their faith would start where they were, Jerusalem, but spread in ever widening circles. Like ripples in water radiating out from the centre, so the gospel would go to Judea, Samaria, and to the ends of the earth. That's what the anointing with the Spirit would enable them to do. Jesus never spoke of giving the Spirit merely to make the disciples feel good, far less for their amusement. Always the gift was for the purpose of equipping them to do God's work. Equally, though, he never imagined anyone trying to do that work without that deep experience of the Spirit.

May God save us today from failing to be the witnesses he wants in a world which so desperately needs his gospel. May God also save us from trying to do that on our own, not allowing his Spirit to permeate our lives and equip us for the task.

Read also: Acts 2:1-4

49
EFFECTIVE PRAYER
(James 5:13-18)

[13]Is any one of you in trouble? He should pray. Is anyone happy? Let him sing songs of praise. [14]Is any one of you sick? He should call the elders of the church to pray over him and anoint him with oil in the name of the Lord. [15]And the prayer offered in faith will make the sick person well; the Lord will raise him up. If he has sinned, he will be forgiven. [16]Therefore confess your sins to each other and pray for each other so that you may be healed. The prayer of a righteous man is powerful and effective.

[17]Elijah was a man just like us. He prayed earnestly that it would not rain, and it did not rain on the land for three and a half years. [18]Again he prayed, and the heavens gave rain, and the earth produced its crops.

Every Christian believes that prayer is essential, yet strangely there's hardly a Christian who could say his prayer life is adequate. It's like someone knowing that good communication is vital for a happy marriage but not managing to talk to his wife more than superficially.

James gives three insights here to help us pray.

1) The naturalness of prayer. Christians can't opt into life's blessings and opt out of life's struggles. But whatever is encountered - trouble, joy, illness, health, sin - James sees prayer as the natural response (verses 13-14). If a child gets top marks in a school exam he runs home to tell his parents. Or, if he falls in the street, tearfully he drags himself back for consolation and a curing kiss. Turning to a father or mother to share something good or find comfort when it's bad is natural for a child. James reckons the Christian can turn just as easily to his heavenly Father. Praise and prayer are meant to be the obvious and natural reaction of the Christian as he faces life's joys and traumas.

2) The certainty of prayer's answer. James has no doubts about prayer. It's never a gesture nor a last grasping after a forlorn hope. Prayer will change things. Healing and forgiveness come by prayer (verses 15 and 16), and Elijah's prayer even stopped rain falling for years (verses 17 and 18). Prayer is answered - that's for sure. When a child rushes through the door just home from school, he shouts, "What's for tea?" There's no hesitant asking whether there will be any tea. He knows there will, because his parents love him and have pledged themselves to provide for him. So there's bound to be tea and all he's asking is what's on tonight's menu. That's the child's confidence in his parents, even though they're not perfect. How sad that people trust other fallible people better than Christians trust their infallible God. James didn't think like that. He was positive about God. "Prayer...is powerful and effective" (verse 16).

3) Relationships affect prayer's effectiveness. James speaks of two relationships. The first is man to man (sometimes called 'the horizontal dimension'), and he says we should confess our sins to each other (verse 16). Broken human relationships must be straightened out so that prayers are unaffected. James is writing about healing, and only God can do that. But, when one person has fallen out with another, God is distanced from that individual. Other New Testament writers teach this too. Peter saw the danger in a bad marriage, and wrote that husbands must respect their wives so that nothing would hinder their prayers (1 Peter 3:7). John went so far as to say that no-one can have a relationship with God while he has a broken relationship with his Christian brother (1 John 4:20 and 21). What lies behind this teaching is the simple truth that someone brought into God's family must have the Father's loving nature flowing into and through him. If that person is living out of fellowship with others there's clearly a break in his fellowship with God. And if he's not in touch with God his prayers won't be answered.

The other important relationship James describes is with God himself (the vertical dimension). Powerful and effective prayers come from "a righteous man" (verse 16). Does that mean only good people get their prayers answered? Certainly the Bible teaches that those who live against God will get nowhere with their prayers (Isaiah 59:1-2). However, if answers to prayer were a reward for goodness then there would be none since God's only acceptable standard is perfection. Thankfully the Bible does not teach that answered prayer depends on merit, or at least not on our merit. What makes us righteous is forgiveness (verse 15). Sins are confessed and then they're gone for ever. Jesus took our badness and gave us his goodness. And so - with the merit of Jesus who lived the perfect life - someone may come before God and be heard. Effective prayer needs that daily confession of sin and trust in Jesus.

Read also: Matthew 6:5-15

50
LETTING GO, LETTING GOD
(Psalm 35:1-3)

¹Contend, O Lord, with those who contend with me;
fight against those who fight against me.
²Take up shield and buckler;
arise and come to my aid.
³Brandish spear and javelin
against those who pursue me.
Say to my soul,
"I am your salvation."

Many people turn their praying into preaching. This Psalmist - probably David - is doing that, but to no audience other than himself (and God!). He's trying to convince his heart to let go of his troubles and trust God to deal with them.

David's problems were many. His life was in danger because enemies had gone to war against him. The situation was bleak. The most natural thing for him to do was arm himself and set out to fight.

But his prayer shows the realisation that that was not the way. David had been anointed by God to be King over Israel. His life was in God's hands. Therefore, although it was a struggle for him to let go of the initiative and trust God, that's what he must do. Let God be the one to "contend" with his enemies. Let God put on his armour, take up his spear, and go to war. And let God speak firmly into David's soul the message: "I am your salvation." David's future depended now on God.

How necessary that lesson still is. How we need God to whisper into *our* souls, "I am your salvation." That's true on the grandest scale of having our sins forgiven and being given new life in Christ. It's equally necessary on the smaller scale of everyday worries about business, relationships, health, finance, guidance, and so on. Our constant temptation is to try and take charge ourselves. We feel we must manage our own lives, and we set out to solve our difficulties using our own resources: education, upbringing, talents, wealth, influence. But that way we achieve little that lasts.

A man sets out for a swim in the sea, foolishly only a short time after a heavy meal. He's out two hundred yards from the beach when severe cramp catches him. He's doubled up in agony, unable to swim to safety. He begins to go under. At that moment what use to him is his luxury car parked by the shore? What help are his three degrees from university? What will his carefully groomed upbringing do for him? None of these matter now. What he needs is to be seen and rescued by the lifeguard. Nothing else will save him.

The sooner we get a parallel perspective on life, realising our dependency on God, the sooner we'll give up finding security in the miscellany of niceties with which we clutter our lives. Instead we'll begin the life of trust in God to which we've been called. 'Let go and let God' will become our motto.

Read also: 2 Chronicles 20:12-18

51
CHRISTIAN MARRIAGE
(Genesis 2:18-24)

[18]The Lord God said, "It is not good for the man to be alone. I will make a helper suitable for him."

[19]Now the Lord God had formed out of the ground all the beasts of the field and all the birds of the air. He brought them to the man to see what he would name them; and whatever the man called each living creature, that was its name. [20]So the man gave names to all the livestock, the birds of the air and all the beasts of the field.

But for Adam no suitable helper was found. [21]So the Lord God caused the man to fall into a deep sleep; and while he was sleeping, he took one of the man's ribs and closed up the place with flesh. [22]Then the Lord God made a woman from the rib he had taken out of the man, and he brought her to the man.

[23]The man said,

> *"This is now bone of my bones*
> *   and flesh of my flesh;*
> *she shall be called 'woman',*
> *   for she was taken out of man."*

[24]For this reason a man will leave his father and mother and be united to his wife, and they will become one flesh.

Much of the New Testament teaching on marriage is based on this section early in Genesis, especially verse 24.

1) Marriage fulfils (verse 18). God saw that it wasn't

good for Adam to be on his own. (Notice: *he* saw that, and *he* decided Adam should have a wife. Marriage was not man's invention and cannot be dropped from society today as outmoded or unnecessary. It was and is God's plan for mankind.) Therefore he would provide him with a helper, not someone identical but a companion who would make Adam a complete person. No creature God had already made could do that, and therefore God specially formed Eve. With her Adam was fulfilled.

Except where there is a special call to singleness, no-one is complete alone. Despite advertisers' promotions of the macho image for men, there's no mileage in the idea of a man as an all-conquering hero who depends on no-one but himself. Nor is there any basis for the feminist portrayal of women as intrinsically independent and self-sufficient, with men irrelevant and inferior. God judged that Adam's life was not whole when he was by himself; neither was Eve meant to have a life separate from Adam. The two needed each other, and could be fulfilled only with each other.

2) Marriage separates (verse 24). It seems strange to think of a marriage, the bonding of two people, involving a separation. But there can be no bond without first a separation. The separation is from the previous bond to parents, or, by implication, to anyone else with whom there has been a committed relationship. A circus entertainer may be able to set thirty or forty plates all spinning on long poles simultaneously, but, if he tries for too many, those which are unattended will begin to crash. Some marriages have failed because other relationships took attention away from the key husband-wife relationship.

No marriage can survive rival attachments. That doesn't mean a couple won't still love and respect their parents, but they will no longer give them the pre-eminence and obedience which they did once. Each will still have loyalties to friends, but never a loyalty to anyone which comes near their loyalty to their marriage partner. Christian marriage is an exclusive relationship. It needs to be, and that means excluding commitments of depth to others.

3) Marriage unites (verse 24). God's arithmetic seems strange: one plus one equals one. Two people marry and become one flesh. Although always different individuals, the marriage union makes them complete in God's eyes to the extent that he considers them one new person. It's almost like what happens when sugar is put into hot tea and stirred: the two elements become one new substance. That's how deeply God regards the joining of a couple in marriage.

No wonder then that God hates divorce (Malachi 2:16; Matthew 19:6). When two are united by God they are not meant to try to prise their marriage apart later. Rather, God's will is for them to find mutual fulfilment in a shared life, and thus to be able to serve him better. Together they can do more than was ever possible when they were independent. They are complete. Now, therefore, they can reach the full potential for which God created them.

Read also: Matthew 19:4-6

52
SPIRITUAL HEALTH CHECK
(1 Timothy 4:6-10)

⁶If you point these things out to the brothers, you will be a good minister of Christ Jesus, brought up in the truths of the faith and of the good teaching that you have followed. ⁷Have nothing to do with godless myths and old wives' tales; rather, train yourself to be godly. ⁸For physical training is of some value, but godliness has value for all things, holding promise for both the present life and the life to come.

⁹This is a trustworthy saying that deserves full acceptance ¹⁰(and for this we labour and strive), that we have put our hope in the living God, who is the Saviour of all men, and especially of those who believe.

The first letter to Timothy reads almost like instructions from a managing director to one of his branch managers on how the business is to be run. The directions, of course, cover topics relevant to leadership of a church: false teachers, worship, qualifications needed in senior staff (overseers and deacons), care of the needy, warnings on temptation, and other matters. They all concern how Timothy is to go about being a successful manager (pastor).

Chapter four, however, is different in tone and content. Here the director shows concern for the well-being of his branch manager. By encouragement and command Paul checks that Timothy's life is in good order so that he's able to run the business. He's asking, "By the way, how are you? Are you coping these days?" Paul wants Timothy to be "a good minister of Christ Jesus" (verse 6). He's checking his spiritual health. He wants his helper to be fit. Was he?

1) His upbringing had been good. It may be depressing for those over the age of about five, but medical scientists are discovering that the essentials which determine good or bad health for us as adults are laid down in childhood. For example, many of the major contributory factors to coronary heart disease, such as lack of exercise and an inadequate diet, are decided long before we've reached adulthood and bought our first book on jogging. A right upbringing is vital for health.

Paul believed the same was true for spiritual health, so he was encouraged that Timothy had been "brought up in the truths of the faith and of the good teaching that you have followed" (verse 6).

People aren't well if they eat junk food. Paul saw many in his day consuming spiritual junk. The very next verse warns against "godless myths and old wives' tales". Some of those he details earlier in the chapter - rules forbidding marriage and teaching abstinence from certain foods. At best these things were a waste of time; at worst they were misleading and dangerous. Perhaps Paul would feel much the same today about arguments which can divide churches, some over patterns of worship (even over which hymn book should be used) and others about how and when Christ's second coming will happen. While we fight each other a world perishes through not hearing the elementary truths of the faith. Paul saw deceiving spirits as the origin of some of the debates of his day (verse 1). Could any of ours have the same source?

Timothy had spiritual health because all along he had fed on the important truths and good teaching.

2) The goodness was ongoing. The word in verse 6 translated 'brought up' is interesting. Firstly, the basic meaning of *entrepho* has to do with being nourished on or sustained by something. Secondly, Paul uses the present participle of the verb, so he is describing an ongoing activity, not one which is finished.

Put these two factors together, and the verse could be translated, "If you point these things out to the brothers, you will be a good minister of Christ Jesus, constantly nourished on the truths of the faith and of the good teaching that you have followed." In other words, his development isn't finished. While Timothy is giving out to others, he is continually to be taking in fresh resources for himself.

After a wonderful party, when the food has tempted the eyes beyond the stomach's capacity to contain, people recline in soft chairs, unable to move. With a contented sigh they mutter, "I won't need to eat again for a week!" But they do. The body is designed for a regular intake of nourishment, not binges on every seventh day.

Neither did God design us for spiritual binges on every seventh day. Nowhere in Scripture is anyone encouraged to have a Sunday-only relationship with God. The Bible reading, prayers, and commitment of that day are not meant to last through until the next week.

Sadly, for some the distance between periods of spiritual experience are even longer. They say, "I had a tremendous Christian experience when I was younger." Or, "I did a Bible correspondence course five years ago." Paul would be unimpressed. He'd want to know what nourishment is being taken from the truths of the faith and good teaching now - not last week, not five years ago, not back in childhood. If someone did eat only one large meal and then nothing else whatsoever for a whole seven days, without question that person would be in a very weak and fragile condition, unable to do much physically. When we find ourselves so impotent spiritually, lacking the power and dynamism possessed by New Testament Christians, could the reason be a failure to have a sustained, daily, living relationship with Jesus?

A good, ongoing development of our Christian lives is essential for spiritual fitness. Timothy had that on top of the right foundation of truth. He could pass Paul's health check. Could we?

Read also: Philippians 3:10-4:1

53
FEAR OF GOD
(Jeremiah 5: 19-22a, 29-31)

[19]*"And when the people ask, 'Why has the Lord our God done all this to us?' you will tell them, 'As you have forsaken me and served foreign gods in your own land, so now you will serve foreigners in a land not your own.'*

[20]*"Announce this to the house of Jacob*
and proclaim it in Judah:
[21]*Hear this, you foolish and senseless people,*
who have eyes but do not see,
who have ears but do not hear:
[22]*Should you not fear me?" declares the Lord.*
"Should you not tremble in my presence?..."

[29]*"Should I not punish them for this?"*
declares the Lord.
"Should I not avenge myself
on such a nation as this?
[30]*"A horrible and shocking thing*
has happened in the land:
[31]*The prophets prophesy lies,*
the priests rule by their own authority,
and my people love it this way.
But what will you do in the end?"

God cannot be taken by surprise. He knows past, present, and future, so misses nothing. Yet, here are people in Jeremiah's day who live as if God is deaf and blind to what they're doing. Their behaviour suggests God might as well not exist. And that's unacceptable. " 'Should you not fear me?' declares the Lord. 'Should you not tremble in my presence?'" (verse 22) His words express astonishment at their attitude. God would have expected them to fear him. Why? We can answer that by asking in general terms what it is that someone fears.

1) He fears only that in which he believes. Most mothers have had the experience of finally slumping in the favourite armchair after the long struggle to settle down a child, only to hear loud wailing within minutes. Back to the little monster she goes.

"What's the matter?"

"You put the light out and now I'm frightened of ghosties," comes the sobbing reply. And the poor exhausted parent has to comfort the child. If she can't dispel the idea of ghosts she may have to resort to leaving on the light!

Because of silly playground chatter or not-so-harmless television programmes, this child believes in the existence of creatures who will harm him in the dark. Therefore he's afraid. The adult knows better. She doesn't believe in them, so isn't afraid and when her head hits the pillow nothing will keep the worn out mother awake. Such are the joys of parenthood...

Clearly, fear depends on belief.

2) He fears only that which he believes can harm him. Silly stories breed in the school playground. So do bullies. Many children are afraid of a tough, older child who throws his weight around.

But who's afraid of the youngest and tiniest shrimp in the school? The peas served at school lunches rival his muscles for size. He poses no threat. No-one runs from him.

So, fear exists only where there is also the belief that something or someone can do harm.

3) He fears only that which he believes will harm him. While a husband lies asleep in bed, there's little to stop his wife creeping downstairs, selecting the longest knife from the kitchen, and then returning to dispatch him to an early grave. But do most husbands lie awake afraid of that? Hopefully not. In a good relationship both go off to sleep feeling content and safe because of the other's love.

A person fears only someone or something he believes will harm him.

Through the prophet, God expresses surprise at this people's lack of fear precisely because of these elements.

The first applied. Undoubtedly they believed in God. They were even aware that much of their suffering was from him, because they were asking, "Why has the Lord our God done all this to us?" (verse 19). Their belief in God's existence was beyond question.

The second applied. If ever a people were conscious of their history it was the Jews. Over and over they had seen God discipline them when they stepped out of line. From the early days of manufacturing a golden calf and hesitating about entering the Promised Land they'd experienced the strong hand of God bringing correction. That's why they realised that their present troubles must be from him. They knew what God could do.

So now they should fear God. If the first two principles are true, that the God in whom they believed could bring punishment on disobedient people, the third element offers no comfort. God had not hesitated to use hard discipline before. The principle that you should fear only that which you believe will harm you ought to have stopped them in their tracks and made them change fast. Otherwise they were in dire trouble.

They had not been following God and living holy lives. They'd been serving false gods (verse 19), with prophets lying and priests usurping authority (verse 31). God had seen that and knew his people were not merely victims of bad leadership. His conclusion was, "...my people love it this way" (verse 31).

So God asks, in wonder: "Should you not fear me? Should you not tremble in my presence?" (verse 22). Had not the people learned that God could not and would not turn a blind eye to idolatry and injustice?

And he wouldn't ignore their sin out of love for them. When a parent sees his child dash across the road without pausing first to check for traffic, at the least that parent gives a stern lecture. He may also apply a rear-end reminder to help the lecture sink in. Is he being cruel? Is he lacking in love? No, precisely the opposite. Because he loves his son and doesn't want him to die in a traffic accident he must discipline him so he learns to obey the rules of the road, rules which will preserve his life. Likewise with God. He loved his people so much he wouldn't let them drift on and on to disaster.

His final question to them is, "...what will you do in the end?" (verse 31). The child will die on the road unless he learns the rules which help him live. As things stand these people are heading for an eternal death. Whatever it takes - even punishment - they must learn to fear God. If they will, and if they will learn their appropriate rules of loving and following this God, then, "in the end" they will find eternal life.

Read also: John 15:1-10

54
BUILT TO LAST
(Matthew 7:24-27)

²⁴Therefore everyone who hears these words of mine and puts them into practice is like a wise man who built his house on the rock. ²⁵The rain came down, the streams rose, and the winds blew and beat against that house; yet it did not fall, because it had its foundation on the rock. ²⁶But everyone who hears these words of mine and does not put them into practice is like a foolish man who built his house on sand. ²⁷The rain came down, the streams rose, and the winds blew and beat against that house, and it fell with a great crash.

These houses had several things in common, and one very fundamental difference.

Both looked good. Whether we should imagine these homes were great mansions or merely small apartments, there's no reason to suppose that their outward appearance was other than impressive. Each owner would build his home with care.

Both were in attractive locations. Some prefer the spectacular view from a cliff; some like to be right on the shore. No estate agent, though, would have had much trouble parting with either of these properties. They were well situated for popular appeal.

Both experienced the same storms. Neither escaped the drenching of the rain, the roar of the river, and the buffeting of the wind. Each suffered appalling weather.

Only one still stood at the end. Only one had had a solid foundation laid into rock, and only it survived. The sand under the other would be swept away in the gales, and with the sand went the house built on it.

Many people's lives look very impressive. They have good backgrounds, great talents, and promising careers. They wear beautiful clothes, own luxury appliances and furniture, and drive expensive cars. Outwardly there's little with which to find fault. Life should be good.

And it is...until the storms come. Then, what good a great career when health is failing? What use fine furniture when a loved one has walked out on the marriage? What purpose a great education when called to account to a holy God?

All may face such storms. When they come the one who has lived in obedience to Jesus finds comfort, strength, and mercy. He or she doesn't have an escape from the storm, but is still *standing* when it's over. Others knew Jesus' words but avoided doing them. That saved them time, effort, and sacrifice, and gave them some short term gains. But the storm's force showed there was no secure foundation. All they'd worked for was destroyed.

To build a life that lasts involves knowing Jesus' words and putting them into practice.

Read also: Revelation 3:14-22

55
TAKING ROOT
(Colossians 1:3-8)

³We always thank God, the Father of our Lord Jesus Christ, when we pray for you, ⁴because we have heard of your faith in Christ Jesus and of the love you have for all the saints -⁵the faith and love that spring from the hope that is stored up for you in heaven and that you have already heard about in the word of truth, the gospel ⁶that has come to you. All over the world this gospel is bearing fruit and growing, just as it has been doing among you since the day you heard it and understood God's grace in all its truth. ⁷You learned it from Epaphras, our dear fellow-servant, who is a faithful minister of Christ on our behalf, ⁸and who also told us of your love in the Spirit.

There are some people who seem naturally to look on the down side of life. They find little for which to be grateful. Paul is not one of those, and usually he finds plenty for which to be thankful. That's particularly so when he thinks of these Colossian Christians. In verses 3 and 4 here, he gives particular thanks to God for two things about them.

1) For their faith in Jesus. News of their belief has reached Paul, and that excites and thrills his heart. Nothing could be more important than that they should have faith in the Saviour. It is the fundamental.

That news has come from Epaphras who is also the one who brought the gospel to these Colossians (verses 7 and 8). Paul is happy to consider Epaphras a "dear fellow-servant" and "a faithful minister of Christ" (verse 7). He's someone Paul trusts, a colleague in the evangelistic work. Because he was the one who sowed the seed, Paul can have confidence that a good job will have been done. This harvest is for real. Their faith will be genuine.

All over the world then, and in Colosse in particular, there is a harvest (verse 6). So he's thankful.

Paul had many problems as an apostle. Many a city rejected his ministry, often persecuting him with considerable violence. (2 Corinthians 11:23-33 describes some of Paul's immense troubles.) Some fellow-workers let him down; some converts fell away. Despite all his difficulties, though, he never lost his gratitude for the many good things God was doing on both a local and international scale. Yes, there were setbacks. But God's word was still spreading everywhere, and what had happened at Colosse was one tangible example of that.

Many today could do with that more positive approach. They should lift their eyes off the struggles of Christian faith and of the church, and see that Paul's words of verse 6 are still true, that all over the world the gospel is bearing fruit and growing. If only they noticed that God's church worldwide is growing faster today than at any time, then they too would find plenty reasons to be thankful.

2) For their love for fellow Christians. Paul notes carefully the love these Colossian Christians show, mentioning it in verses 4, 5 and 8. Along with faith, he regards love as an essential part of the gospel.

So did other New Testament writers. Both James and John were convinced that real faith would always be revealed in practical care (e.g., James 2:14-26; 1 John 4:19-21). It's bound to be so. The natural response of people who realise how much God has done for them is to reflect his actions in tangible love for others. Also, the Holy Spirit of God, who now lives in his people, is bound to want to show God's love through them to others. Perhaps that's part of Paul's meaning when he speaks of "love in the Spirit" seen in the Colossians.

One of the challenges to today's Christians is to show this godly love to others. Christians all too easily distance themselves, seeming aloof and judgmental. Had God behaved like that toward us, then Jesus would never have left heaven. Instead, in love, he came to save the very people who lived against him. He cared enough to give his life for us. Those in whom his Spirit lives will likewise give themselves sacrificially to care for others.

For Paul, that was another evidence of the reality of these Colossians' faith. They had believed the gospel; their love for others was proof that that belief was not merely superficial seed but something which had taken deep root in their lives. So Paul was thankful.

Today, wherever there is faith and love let's recognise God has been at work. And whenever that's happened there is every reason for thankfulness.

Read also: Matthew 22:34-40

56
WHAT IS GOD LIKE?
(Psalm 42:1-2)

¹As the deer pants for streams of water,
so my soul pants for you, O God.
²My soul thirsts for God, for the living God.
When can I go and meet with God?

Most people about to meet someone for the first time like
to know a little in advance what he's like. There's no
reason why that should be any different for someone like
this Psalmist who wants to meet God.

Since God is spirit (that is, with no physical form), we
can only describe him in terms of his nature and behaviour.
Here are three key characteristics about God.

1) He is perfect. Things we do are a mixture of good and
bad. The schoolboy occasionally gets his sums right and
often gets them wrong. The driver sometimes keeps to the
Highway Code, and other times lets the standard slip. The
cook gets some recipes just right, but many times what's
served doesn't look as it did in the picture.

With God there's no mixture. Nothing he does is sub-
standard. His work in creation was exactly as he meant it
to be: "God saw all that he had made, and it was very good"
(Genesis 1:31). The laws he gave his people were just in
every detail: "The law of the Lord is perfect, reviving the
soul" (Psalm 19:7). Everything about his nature and behaviour is right, as Jesus said: "Be perfect, the
your heavenly Father is perfect" (Matthe
no flaws, no weak points, no bad tra

2) God is moral. That may seem obvious, but in fact it is a crucial characteristic of God. Abraham knew that, so could ask the rhetorical question, "Will not the Judge of all the earth do right?" (Genesis 18:25).

Such a God, then, distinguishes right from wrong, he only does what is right, and defines wrongness in others by comparison with his own actions. That last point could be likened to a maths teacher marking his pupils' exam papers by comparison with his own sheet of correct answers. He lays each pupil's paper alongside his own, and thus has a standard by which he can judge the answers of that pupil. Similarly, God's perfect morality reveals where we go wrong.

3) God is loving. The apostle John said simply, "God is love" (1 John 4:8). Sure enough, from ancient times those who had dealings with God found he was tender and good to them. The Psalmist described God as the one "who forgives all your sins and heals all your diseases, who redeems your life from the pit and crowns you with love and compassion... The Lord is compassionate and gracious, slow to anger, abounding in love... For as high as the heavens are above the earth, so great is his love for those who fear him... As a father has compassion on his children, so the Lord has compassion on those who fear him..." (Psalm 103:3,4,8,11,13). Every experience of God showed him to be loving.

If you buy a raspberry cane you can be sure it'll produce raspberries. It won't produce blackberries or any other kind, because its 'nature' defines what fruit it will bear. Likewise, a God who is love will act always in loving ways.

So God is perfect, moral, and loving. Of course, if he is then he is entitled to pass judgment on us. He has has a perfect perspective by which to assess our lives. And, if he is moral then he will judge us. A moral God cannot allow sin to go forever unchecked in his universe. If there were no reliability standard for cars (the dreaded MOT test), and any vehicle in any condition could be on the roads, then accident after accident would happen as brakes failed, steering racks snapped, and cars with no lights crashed. The roads would become a scene of disaster. In the same way, if God overlooked sin there would be spiritual anarchy. A moral God will not allow that.

It sounds like bad news that God can and will judge people like us who fall so far short of his perfect morality. The good news is that because he is also love, he sent his only Son to take the penalty for our sin. He bore that on himself when he accepted a death sentence on the cross on our behalf. Our wrongness was given to him; his goodness was given to us.

Joe Bloggs has a wreck of an old car which will never pass the official safety test. Fred Soap's car, by contrast, is immaculate. Out of a loving and generous heart, Fred says to Joe, "I'll swap cars with you. Take mine as your own and I'll keep the one you had." Joe's dream has come true. Of course the immaculate car he has now sails through the test without a problem. Joe has inherited a heap of junk, and to the junkyard it goes after failing the test. He has taken Fred's loss for him.

So it was that Jesus Christ took our sinful failures on himself all the way to a scrapheap called Calvary. There he suffered, and died for them. Now all who accept the gift of his perfect life will pass God's strictest test. The perfect, moral and loving God gives his people the salvation they could never achieve themselves. That's what he's like.

Read also: 1 John 4:7-10

57
THE JUDGMENT NET
(Matthew 13:47-50)

⁴⁷Once again, the kingdom of heaven is like a net that was let down into the lake and caught all kinds of fish. ⁴⁸When it was full, the fishermen pulled it up on the shore. Then they sat down and collected the good fish in baskets, but threw the bad away. ⁴⁹This is how it will be at the end of the age. The angels will come and separate the wicked from the righteous ⁵⁰and throw them into the fiery furnace, where there will be weeping and gnashing of teeth.

Some of Jesus' parables are stark and forceful. No-one could miss his meaning. That's certainly true with this parable of the net in which Jesus is speaking of judgment.

1) Judgment is of all. The net Galilean fishermen used didn't discriminate between types of fish. It had a fine mesh, and every sea creature in its path was caught and hauled to shore. None escaped through the net.

And no-one escapes judgment. In this life plenty things make a difference to what we have to do: looks, wealth, influence, education, talent, race, etc. But these count for nothing at judgment time. Everyone, no matter what, will be caught up in that experience.

2) Judgment separates. Having caught everything, the fishermen of Jesus' day still had to sort through their fish after they had dragged their net to shore. Some were kept; others were thrown away. Jesus uses that fact bluntly. It pictures the radical separation of those fit for God's kingdom from those who are not. There will be a division.

All will experience judgment, but not all will experience the same result from that judgment.

3) Judgment is definite. Most things in life are contingent on circumstances. Someone may marry, but only if he meets the right person. Another may be famous, but only if he's a talented singer, sportsman, or something similar. A third may be rich, but only if he has a large income, inherits wealth, or wins some great prize. For all of us plenty things may happen, but few are definite. Almost the only thing that is sure is that one day we'll die, and after that will come judgment (Hebrews 9:27). This separation will happen. "This is how it will be at the end of the age," says Jesus. There's no doubt about that.

4) Judgment is terrible for some. Artists and writers have portrayed hell as a place where evil pleasures are satiated. Jesus pictures nothing pleasurable at all about it. His image is of a red hot furnace where people weep and gnash their teeth. Precisely what hell is like no-one can imagine. The indescribable is put into the nearest equivalent terms, and clearly it's a place of terror and misery.

How sad, then, that so many point their lives in hell's direction. Since all will be judged and the stakes are so high - heaven or hell - it makes sense to choose now to be part of the good catch. That involves faith in Jesus as Saviour and obeying him as Lord. All who follow him are given his righteousness, the essential element for entry into heaven.

Many imagine they're good enough to earn a place in heaven, and think little if at all about Jesus. One day they'll discover that what they considered so good was far less than God's standard (Romans 3:23). Sadly most will find that out only when they're caught in God's judgment net, and by then it'll be too late to escape.

Read also: 2 Corinthians 5:6-10

58
WHO KNOWS?
(John 10:14-16)

¹⁴I am the good shepherd; I know my sheep and my sheep know me - ¹⁵just as the Father knows me and I know the Father - and I lay down my life for the sheep. ¹⁶I have other sheep that are not of this sheep pen. I must bring them also. They too will listen to my voice, and there shall be one flock and one shepherd.

What Jesus says in each of these three verses is essential knowledge for those who take him seriously. All of it has to do with his role as the good shepherd.

1) Know and be known by the good shepherd (verse 14). Some think everyone belongs to Jesus, even if they pay him no heed. They believe every person in the world is his, that somehow they're Christians without knowing it. Such 'universalist' ideas are nonsense when compared with these words of Jesus. He says sheep and shepherd quite definitely know each other.

What kind of marriage could there be if one person neither knew nor was committed to the other person? It's unthinkable. And Jesus sets man's first priority as entering into a personal relationship with him. Without knowing him and being known by him there is no belonging to this flock.

2) Know that this good shepherd has died in your place (verse 15). Earlier verses point out that a hired hand runs away when a wolf attacks. He cares nothing for the sheep he's supposed to guard. But this good shepherd cares to the point of death.

Imagine a wolf attempting to prey on a flock of sheep. Just as he is about to leap on the weak and helpless animals to despatch them to a swift and nasty end, the shepherd puts himself in the way. He takes the fangs and the gouging claws, allowing the sheep meanwhile to make their escape. Thus, for the sake of his sheep, the shepherd dies in their place. He did not need to. He chose to. Such was his love.

3) Know that the good shepherd still searches for his other sheep (verse 16). This shepherd means to gather many more sheep into his flock. For the moment they're still lost, but he wants them found. All that belong to his flock should be at his side, the place of safety. There is an urgency here: "I must bring them also." There can be no thought of abandoning them or waiting before gathering them in.

Originally Jesus' words meant finding 'sheep' outside the nation of Israel. Today Christ's sheep are still scattered all through his world. Christians must go seeking them wherever they are. The Holy Spirit drives those who already know the shepherd to find those who don't. The encouraging promise of this verse is that when those other sheep hear of him they too will listen to his voice.

That seeking must go on today and every day. It's a task which will not be finished until the day when there is one flock, a complete flock, alongside the one good shepherd.

Read also: Matthew 18:12-14

59
FACE THE FACTS
(1 Timothy 1:15)

Here is a trustworthy saying that deserves full acceptance:
Christ Jesus came into the world to save sinners - of whom I
am the worst.

This is known as one of the 'faithful sayings' of Paul's
pastoral letters. In a few words he captures the heart of the
gospel. The simplest way to grasp his message is to put a
few direct questions to the verse.

1) Who? Who came? Who came to save sinners? Paul's
answer is "Christ Jesus".

And no-one else is mentioned. Had he been writing
today, his answer would never have been Jesus, Buddha,
Krishna, Mohammed, or any other of a series of modern
prophets. Jesus is not one among many. Jesus, and only
Jesus, came to save sinners.

If someone has a terminal illness and hears that there is
only one consultant with a cure, a man living at the other
end of the earth, to whom does he go for treatment? Is it
to his local GP? Is it to the specialist at his neighbourhood
hospital? These people may have their merits, but if the
man is determined to be healed then he books a flight and
heads to the one consultant with a cure. And consistently
the Bible teaches there is only one man with the cure for
sins, Jesus of Nazareth. We waste our time and energy
looking to anyone else for forgiveness.

2) Where? Where did he come? Paul says Jesus "came
into the world" when he wanted to save sinners.

He had to. God could have sat in heaven and warned men of their behaviour, sent down more laws, even given them more time to change, but ultimately none of these would have removed man's sentence of death for sin. What was needed was someone without sin of his own to take man's sin on himself and suffer man's death for him. But only a man could take man's penalty. Therefore the Son of God became a man, and died in our place. He came from heaven to earth to save sinners.

3) Why? Why did Jesus come? He came "to save".

If you judged by many people's reaction to Jesus - ranging from no more than polite respect through to out-right hostility - you would think he'd come to do something irrelevant or even harmful. In fact he hung on our cross for us.

A man finds himself overdrawn at the bank. He's written rubber cheques which bounced their way back to him, and now the debt collectors are at the door. Soon his furniture and even his home will be sold to pay what he owes. At that critical moment the postman brings a letter from a dear old aunt. Inside is a cheque! The man stares in astonishment at a row of zeros. She's giving him a gift of thousands of pounds. So what does he do? Does he throw it in a drawer and forget about it? Does he post it back with a stiff note telling her to keep her charity? Not likely. The man immediately gets that cheque into his account so that her money can pay his debts. And, of course, he thanks her. It's the least he can do. She's saved him from disaster.

Jesus came to save us forever from a lost eternity. He doesn't deserve hostility or indifference. Polite respect is equally inadequate. His sacrifice deserves a response of faith, and loving gratitude in worship and a life of service.

4) Whom? This is another 'who?' question, but directed

differently. **Whom did Jesus come to save?** The answer is that he came to save "sinners".

That's all of us. Some have done better than others, but none have loved God with all their heart, soul, and mind (Matthew 22:37). Everyone falls short of his standard (Romans 3:23). But the good news Paul brings is that we're not rejected or abandoned by God. Jesus came to save sinners.

Paul knew how much he needed Jesus. He felt he was the worst sinner of all time because he had persecuted Christians in his former life as a Pharisee (described in Acts 8:1-3). Yet Jesus saved even him. Therefore there was hope for anyone.

And there is. If the only qualification to be saved is to be a sinner, then we're all included. What remains is the equivalent of the bankrupt man cashing the cheque. The gift of money only helped him when he accepted it into his account. Likewise Jesus died for sinners, and invites our acceptance of him now as Saviour.

This is Paul's 'faithful saying'- key facts which will faithfully lead those who heed them to new life in Jesus.

Read also: Luke 5:27-32

60
KNOWN THROUGH AND THROUGH
(Psalm 139:1-4)

¹O Lord, you have searched me
and you know me.
²You know when I sit and when I rise;
you perceive my thoughts from afar.
³You discern my going out and my lying down;
you are familiar with all my ways.
⁴Before a word is on my tongue
you know it completely, O Lord.

The message here is that God knows us through and through. Nothing about us is hidden from God. Our movements, thoughts, and words are all plain to him. We can pretend with others, letting them see only our good side. But we can't pretend with God. He knows us as we know ourselves.

Indeed, he knows us better than that. Verse 4 says that while we're still thinking up words, God already is aware of what we will say. We see only our present and our past. God also discerns our future. It's as if God has X-ray eyes to see through us at every level. Nothing about us is secret to him.

All of this is a remarkable example of the power of God. What is even more remarkable is that God still loves us. He knows everything and still cares. The worst sin of our past; the desperate doubts of the present; the evil we may yet do in the future; none of that is lost on him. But it makes no difference.

People fear they may fall out of the love of God, that something will arise to kill off his friendship. That idea comes from human relationships, where people can be hurt to such a degree that they 'go off' someone. There are differences in a relationship with God, however. Partly that's because of his utter consistency of character. He doesn't have whims. But also there's the point emerging here, that nothing we do catches him by surprise. Before he ever decided to love us, he knew what we were like, and knew what we would be like. Nothing can come to the surface from our past to rock the relationship. There's nothing we'll do in the future to suddenly offend him and cause him to distance himself.

In the light of what God had already seen in us - past, present, and future - he sent his Son to die in our place and then called us to faith by his Spirit. He did not act in ignorance. He knew us. And still he wanted us.

It would be hard to imagine a relationship with greater security than that. We're known through and through, and still loved.

Read also: Ephesians 1:3-14

INDEX OF
BIBLE PASSAGES

Text		Epilogue no.
MATTHEW	18:21-35	13
	20:18-20	3
MARK	1:14-15	32
	1:16-18	36
	10:17-22	39
LUKE	18:9-14	5
	24:44-53	2
JOHN	3:16-21	9
	10:14-16	58
	10:14-18	46
	10: 27-30	18
ACTS	1:4-5,8	48
	2:42-47	26
	3:1-10	20
	6:1-7	45
ROMANS	1:18-20	28
1 CORINTHIANS	15:12-23	30
PHILIPPIANS	3:12-14	10
COLOSSIANS	1:3-8	55
	3:1-4	31
1 TIMOTHY	1:15	59
	4:6-10	52
	4:7-10	35
2 TIMOTHY	2:11-13	6
JAMES	4:13-17	40
	5:13-18	49
1 PETER	4:10-11	16
	5:6-7	43
REVELATION	3:19-22	21
	20:11-21:4	47